Edible

Series Editor: Andrew F. Smith

EDIBLE is a revolutionary series of books dedicated to food and drink that explores the rich history of cuisine. Each book reveals the global history and culture of one type of food or beverage.

Already published

Dumplings

A Global History

Barbara Gallani

REAKTION BOOKS

To my dumpling-loving family

Published by Reaktion Books Ltd
33 Great Sutton Street
London EC1V 0DX, UK

www.reaktionbooks.co.uk

First published 2015

Printed and bound in China

A catalogue record for this book is available
from the British Library

ISBN 978 1 78023 433 5

Contents

I

What is a Dumpling?

The word 'dumpling' can mean many different things in the culinary world: fluffy balls of wheat flour and animal fat floating to the surface of hearty stews; delicate parcels of dough filled with meat or vegetables and then steamed; or firm little lumps of potato, egg and flour served in a thick sauce. Savoury and sweet dumplings are widespread across the world, with simple varieties served as an everyday meal in the home or in school and factory canteens. More elaborate versions are prepared once or twice a year for celebrations and festivals.

Any official definition of the word 'dumpling' is likely only to partially describe what is an extraordinary variety of foods. This difficulty in finding a universal definition is also caused by the fact that the English word 'dumpling' is used as a shortcut translation for a long list of foods that have very similar characteristics but also very well-defined identities and vocabulary in the language of the country from which they come. The glossary at the end of this book provides an idea of these differences and similarities. A chef in Chiang Mai, Thailand – well-versed in Asian dumplings and in their some-times very subtle differences – once said to me, pointing at a number of bamboo steamers on a dim sum trolley, 'Chinese

Mongolian *buuz* filled with mutton or yak and steamed.

dumplings: same same but different.' This popular Thai saying seemed quite appropriate in the circumstances.

In order to match the meaning of the original language, some translations are required to be less telegraphic than the simple word 'dumpling', and might extend to a fuller description of the food including its ingredients, cooking method and presentation. The single Italian word *carmelle*, for example, captures very succinctly all the following characteristics: a dumpling made of a thin wheat wrap, ricotta cheese and spinach filling, shaped as a wrapped boiled sweet, boiled in water, served with melted butter and sage, and typical of the town of Piacenza, northern Italy. The English translation, correct but far from comprehensive, would simply be 'Italian type of filled dumpling'.

The *Oxford English Dictionary* limits its definition to 'a small savoury ball of dough', excluding other shapes and omitting any reference to the possible presence of a filling. On the other hand, it accepts 'boiled, fried and baked in a casserole' as suitable cooking methods. For the purpose of this book, my definition of a dumpling, which I have developed over many years of research and in-depth conversations with chefs, cooks and enthusiasts, as well as a fair amount of eating, extends to both unfilled and filled varieties, including what is sometimes described as filled pasta. However, I prefer to exclude frying and baking as cooking methods, since these result in what people usually recognize as fritters or small pasties rather than dumplings.

Many unfilled dumplings are very easy to prepare, being nothing more than a few basic ingredients mixed together,

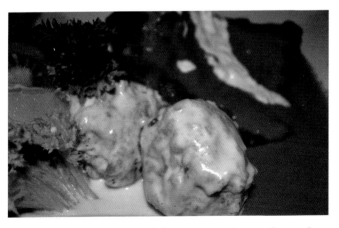

Many unfilled dumplings are simple homogeneous mixtures of a very few common ingredients, cooked in boiling water and served with roasted meat and gravy or stews.

dropped into boiling water, drained and served with a stew or rich sauce. To make things even simpler, they can also be cooked directly in the broth or casserole in which they will be served. This type of dumpling is used to add bulk to a meal and as an alternative to potatoes, pasta or rice. The simplest recipes include just wheat flour and water; other typical ingredients include breadcrumbs and fat, sometimes with the addition of herbs, cheese or egg. In Africa, wheat flour is replaced by millet, yam or other local starchy ingredients, while in Central, Eastern and Northern Europe potatoes tend to be the main ingredient of choice. Unfilled dumplings are not ideally served on their own, since they taste bland and, although filling, are not particularly nutritious.

Filled dumplings consist of a layer of dough wrapped around a seemingly infinite variety of juicy and tasty fillings. There is no limit to the imagination when it comes to possible ingredients, the only constraints being availability – clearly linked to geography and seasonality – and tradition. Also, once the art of preparing and rolling the dough and shaping individual dumplings is mastered, depending on whether the dumplings are intended for a quick and simple everyday meal or for a special occasion, more unusual and elaborate combinations of ingredients and flavours can be developed. Filled dumplings are a complete course in themselves and do not need any substantial accompaniment beside the filling; they are served with the simplest of sauces, or with no sauce at all.

My passion for dumplings has meant that I have enthusiastically tried all the following: meat fillings – beef, pork, mutton, chicken, rabbit, yak, duck; vegetables – cabbage, spinach, nettles, mushrooms, pumpkin, chestnut, fennel, artichokes, onions, seaweed; cheese – blue cheese, ricotta, cream cheese, mozzarella; fish – salmon, pollack; seafood – shrimps, lobster, crab; and sweet varieties including fruit, jam, nuts,

Dumplings are produced on an industrial scale, using machines with inter-changeable moulds that wrap double layers of dough around the filling and transport the finished product on a conveyor belt for packing.

chocolate and chocolate/hazelnut spread. I have not yet cooked or been offered a peanut butter variety, but that does not mean it is not available or worth trying. In short, the rule for choosing a filling is that anything goes. In fact, most dumplings, as with many other traditional dishes, were originally intended as a way of using up leftovers, and many recipes make use of stale bread, breadcrumbs and day-old stews, roast meat or fish, saving the time of preparing the filling and resulting in interesting and unique combinations of flavours.

Preparing filled dumplings from scratch can be a tricky and sticky business. It requires practice and patience and is better achieved with more than just one pair of hands. In fact, it is traditional in many cultures for all women of the same family to gather in the kitchen to make dumplings for the feasts that mark particular celebrations, such as for the Catholic Christmas celebrations in Poland or Italy, the Chinese New Year or the eve of Jewish Yom Kippur. The rolling of the dough, the pounding of the filling and the shaping of the dumplings are of course made less onerous by the convivial atmosphere in the kitchen, the presence of children and the sharing of the latest family news and gossip. This is also the most immediate way of passing down recipes and skills to the younger women in the family, and first-timers are encouraged to persevere even if their initial attempts produce less than optimal results.

Once prepared, dumplings can be dried or frozen in large quantities and are then ready to be cooked, when required, in just a few minutes. Many types of ready-to-cook dumpling are now available from supermarkets, Eastern European delis or Asian stores. They are either packed in vacuum containers with a shelf life of several weeks, or can be bought frozen in large family bags and cooked in boiling water when required. Although the whole experience of making dumplings is worth celebrating and perpetuating, it does clearly take a lot of skill, effort and time. In societies that have changed beyond recognition, where the average time dedicated to cooking a meal barely reaches 30 or 40 minutes, the convenience of pre-packed, tasty, easy-to-cook dumplings is welcome and allows the preparation of fast but healthy and complete meals without having to cook from scratch. Traditional recipes coexist on the shelves of supermarkets with new and seasonal varieties. Italian tortellini, for example, are no longer limited to the traditional Parma ham filling but are made with Spanish chorizo and sundried tomatoes or Swiss Emmenthal cheese and juicy raisins. These combinations are the result of the fusion of regional ingredients into tasty

Different types and shapes of dumplings.

and well-balanced recipes accessible to all thanks to the ever-increasing globalization of food supply.

When talking about dumplings, size definitely matters, as it is a defining characteristic of the different varieties. The largest dumplings are served individually or in twos, and often date back to very old, traditional recipes developed from staple ingredients and leftovers. Central European *gomboc*, African *fufu* and South American *tamales* are impressive in size and certainly good plate-fillers. At the opposite end of the scale, 'dropped' dumplings such as the German or Austrian *Spätzle* and Hungarian *csipetke* are tiny little things made of dough cut into very small pieces and rolled into oblongs before being dropped in boiling water for a few minutes. Such examples are testimony to the fact that the generic word 'dumpling' can only begin to describe the many varieties being dished out day in, day out throughout the world.

2
Dumplings Around the World

The geographical spread of the dumpling covers most of the globe, from the Alpine regions of Europe to the Mongolian steppes; from sub-Saharan Africa to rural Japan; and from the maize fields of Latin America to Chinese communities throughout the world. Dumplings have always coexisted as versions of an unpretentious, filling peasant food, making small amounts of meat stretch far enough to feed large families and communities, or as elaborate, refined parcels of dough, wrapped around delicate fillings and served for special occasions.

When looking at the history of the dumpling, it is possible to draw a historical parallel with the well-known debate about whether Italian spaghetti came before or after Chinese noodles. In fact, some types of filled dumpling carry with them interesting questions that remain largely unanswered: is there a documented link between Italian ravioli, Russian *pelmeni*, Central Asian *manti* and Chinese wontons? To what extent did Marco Polo, or any other Venetian merchant for that matter, play a part in culinary exchange and influence between the spice-rich Far East and the established traditions of European kitchens?

The dumpling has developed independently in many different parts of the world through the use of common ingredients. Travel and commercial exchanges have contributed to

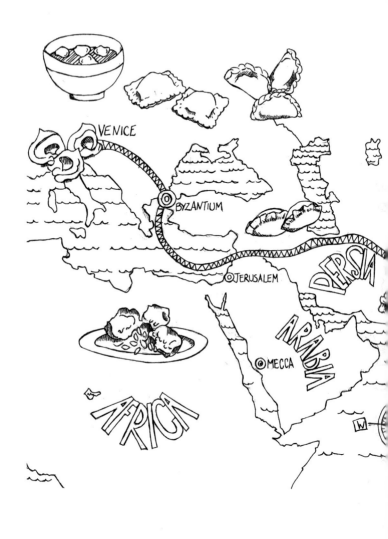

VENICE

BYZANTIUM

JERUSALEM

PERSIA

ARABIA

MECCA

AFRICA

W

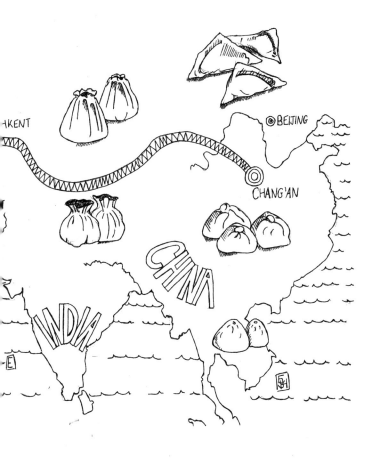

Travel and commercial exchanges along the Silk Road have influenced the evolution of dumplings.

Filled dumplings, including Italian ravioli, are a versatile dish that can be served with very simple sauces or just a drizzle of olive oil.

the transfer of certain shapes and combinations of tastes from country to country and across continents.

The intensive military and commercial activities of the Repubbliche Marinare (the city-states, including Genoa, Pisa and Venice, that flourished in Italy between the tenth and thirteenth centuries) acted as a catalyst for cultural and culinary exchange, as merchants and crusaders alike travelled across the Mediterranean and ventured further into the Middle and Far East than ever before. For example, during the twelfth century ravioli, a square dumpling made of a filling sealed between two layers of thin pasta, began to spread from Genoa to Parma and Venice, and from there to other regions in Europe, in particular through Hungary, Poland and Bohemia. Medieval commercial fairs provided an opportunity for merchants to exchange goods and currencies, and attracted crowds from nearby and faraway towns and villages. Food and drink constituted a big aspect of these commercially motivated and extremely lively gatherings, which owed their popularity also to the presence of acrobats, storytellers, magicians and women of ill repute. The frequent fairs held in Genoa's harbour, then an important centre of commerce in the Mediterranean, certainly played a big role in extending the popularity of ravioli among sailors and merchants from further afield.

In the thirteenth century Genovese and Venetian merchants, including Marco Polo's family, travelled east to conduct commercial dealings and exploration. Marco Polo's account of his incredibly exotic journey, whether fully founded on personal experience or embellished with tales heard along the way, provided inspiration for countless generations of explorers and travellers, as well as insight into the way of life of the nomadic Tartars, or Mongols, including their ceremonies, travels, food and social rules. As Marco Polo was travelling eastwards, the Mongols, led by Ghengis Khan, were

Uzbek *manti*, a staple of Central Asia and the Middle East, served with yoghurt and dill.

Eastern European dumplings such as Polish *pierogi*, Russian *pelmeni* and Ukrainian *varenyky* are very similar in shape, texture and filling.

travelling west across the steppes of Central Asia, conquering neighbouring civilizations and deriving sustenance from dumplings filled with mutton, yak and horse meat, and boiled on open campfires. For Ghengis Khan's Mongols, as for today's Central Asian nomadic populations, meat-based dumplings were an important part of the diet together with dairy products including goat's and mare's milk, cream and cheese.

Central Asia gradually became a melting pot for different traditions of filled dumpling, as commercial exchange and geopolitical developments brought ingredients and recipes from Italy, China and Mongolia into contact with traditional varieties already present in the region. It is notable that in Turkey dumplings are also called *Tatar böregi* (Tartar pasties), and significant common threads across Central Asia are the filling of minced lamb, often charged with black pepper and other spices, and the habit of smothering dumplings in garlic, yoghurt or sour milk.

Claudia Roden, a food writer particularly knowledgeable about Middle Eastern and Jewish cooking, recognizes the strong connection between Italian and Central Asian dumplings in *The Book of Jewish Food: An Odyssey from Samarkand and Vilna to the Present Day* (1997):

> Pasta came to Poland as a result of Italian presence at the royal courts and also by way of Central Asia. That may be why the cheese kreplach [a type of filled dumpling], sauced with sour cream, owes more to the Turkish-Mongolian manti with yoghurt poured over than to Italian ravioli or cappelletti.

The fact that Russian *pelmeni* is filled with a mixture of meats strongly flavoured with black pepper and spices not native to Russia is also often used to corroborate the theory that *pelmeni* originated in China and was carried by the Mongols to Siberia, the Urals and as far as Anatolia and Eastern Europe. However, although influences from the Far East are very plausible, the origin of the Russian dumpling is not clear. One possibility is that it originated in the Urals as pieces of meat wrapped in very thin bread called *pel'nyan'*, which means, in native languages Komi and Mansi, 'bread ear'. It was then spread across Central Asia by Russian explorers and pioneers. It is also possible that it was developed by hunters, who needed light, easy-to-prepare, nourishing food to take with them on long hunting trips. *Pelmeni* fitted the purpose, as it keeps for a long time in sub-zero temperatures and is quickly boiled in pots of water over an open fire.

Other types of dumpling can be found in eastern Europe. These include Ukrainian *varenyky*, which derives its name from the verb 'to boil', and Polish *pierogi*, which is made with various fillings, one of which is practically identical to the Russian dumpling and aptly named *Russkie pierogi*. However, the word *pyrogi*, both in Russia and in Ukraine, describes not a dumpling but a type of fluffy baked bun generally filled with fruit or poppy seeds.

The same phenomenon as that in Central Asia can be easily mapped out across Africa, South America and Northern Europe. In these regions, a variety of very similar unfilled dumplings developed at first independently in different places, making use of common and plentiful ingredients, then spread across each continent, giving rise to interesting hybrid recipes.

On the African continent, unfilled dumplings of similar appearance and taste can be found under different names in a number of countries in the west, east and south. They are a staple and consist of the local carbohydrate source – yam, sweet potato, sorghum, millet, cassava or maize (both originally from South America) – cooked, pounded, shaped into dumplings and served with stewed or roasted meat, fish or vegetables. *Kenkey*, a popular variety in West Africa made of a maize sourdough wrapped in banana leaves and steamed, is equally common in the Caribbean as *mangu* or *mofongo*. In South Africa sweet *souskluitjies* are a favourite among Afrikaans children; these are quite different from dumplings found elsewhere on the continent as they are made with self-raising flour, egg and milk, boiled in plenty of water and served in a very sweet cinnamon syrup.

In Latin America where the staple food is maize, dumplings – either filled (with meat, cheese or raisins and dried fruit) or unfilled – are made with *masa*, a dough of maize flour and

Polish potato balls with meat and pumpkin filling.

Hungarian *knodli* with chicken and paprika stew.

limewater, wrapped in banana leaves and steamed. The name
varies from *tamales* to *humitas*, depending on the country.

In Central and Northern Europe, where one of the main
sources of carbohydrate is the potato, the tuber is boiled and
mashed, or grated when still raw, and then combined into
dumplings bound by egg, fat or milk. Dumplings are then
shaped into balls or ellipses and boiled in water. Although very
similar, they have many different names, in various languages
and local dialects, that often mean 'potato ball', 'potato cake'
or 'potato dumpling'. Some examples are Norwegian *potet klub*
and *potetball*, Polish *kopytka*, German *Kartoffelkloesse* and Danish
frikasseboller.

Jewish dumplings also developed a distinct identity through
the interaction of Jewish communities with ingredients, foods
and traditions around the world, mainly in different parts of
Europe and the Middle East, following the diaspora. The

24

best-known Jewish dumplings are the unfilled *knaidl* (matzah balls) and the filled *kreplach*. Claudia Roden writes:

> The Yiddish word *knaidl* is derived from the German *Knödel*, meaning 'dumpling'. Since the early Middle Ages, dumplings of all kinds have been popular in German, Czech and Austrian cooking, and came into the Jewish diet. All over Eastern Europe they epitomize the robust peasant and poor man's food.
>
> Stuffed pasta shaped like giant cappelletti or tortellini came to the Jews of Germany through Venice in the early fourteenth century.

The birthplace of Asian dumplings is China, where the thousands of combinations of different shapes, fillings and

The Dumpling Seller, *c.* 1790, watercolour and ink on paper, Guangzhou, China. This painting is from a set of 100 that depict different trades and occupations in Canton. Paintings such as this were made for Europeans eager to find out more about China.

recipes can be broadly grouped into three types: wontons, *jiaozi* and *baozi*. Because of the difficulty of transliteration and translation, not to mention regional differences that are sometimes substantial and sometimes very subtle, it is difficult to summarise in a few words the traits of these Chinese specialities. However, the following should serve as a very general description: wonton is made of a very thin dough wrapper and usually served in a broth or steamed. *Jiaozi* are made of a thick and chewy dough, and shaped like a horn or a big Brazil nut. It is usually steamed or boiled and served with a soy-based or hot chilli dip; pan-fried *jiaozi* are known as *guotie* (pot-stickers). *Baozi* are filled buns made of a fluffy, bread-like dough and steamed. In certain parts of China they are called *mantou*, although the name *mantou* mainly refers to plain, unfilled *baozi*.

From China, the wonton travelled west through the Mongolian steppes and east to Korea before crossing the sea, and became a popular staple food in Japan under the name

Chinese pan-fried *jiaozi*, or pot-stickers, are richly flavoured with garlic.

gyoza. At the same time the *baozi* also travelled and became established, under different names, in other Far Eastern countries and as far as Hawaii. The Hawaiian version is known as *manapua* and was brought to these Pacific islands by Chinese migrants in search of work, who started selling it on the streets, initially walking around with baskets of steaming filled dumplings and then selling from vans parked at street corners and on popular beaches. Now *manapua* is also available in bakeries, restaurants and supermarkets.

As is the case with the Chinese dumplings in Hawaii, many food exchanges are a direct consequence of the historical and economic factors that are behind migration. With migrant populations come suitcases and trunks, soon followed by crates and containers, of traditional foods from their countries and regions of origin. For example, dumplings became an established food in North America after migrants from Italy, Germany and other parts of Central and Eastern Europe reached the New World at the same time as waves of migrants from China and other Asian countries. It is curious that in the USA 'ravs', originally an Italo-American contraction of the word ravioli, became a common term sloppily extended to cover any type of filled dumpling that came from outside the country, irrespective of whether it is Italian ravioli, Polish *pierogi* or Russian *pelmeni*. In addition, Chinese wontons are often referred to in the USA as Chinese or Peking ravs.

The fascinating phenomenon of ingredient swapping and cross-referencing between cooking traditions and recipes continues today. Contemporary twists to traditional recipes are more and more common thanks to increased global sourcing of ingredients and foods, affordable travel and immediate access to information. The result is a continuous revision, adaptation and mutation of traditional recipes with a marked impact on regional and local cuisines. For example, cream

Stuffing meat into Chinese-style *baozi* before steaming in large wooden baskets for large-scale production.

cheese wontons are now served in North American Chinese restaurants, and Mars bar and Nutella *momo* (a boiled dumpling traditionally filled with mutton or vegetables) is very popular with homesick, chocolate-craving backpackers in cafés across Nepal and Tibet.

3
Etymology, Historical Documents and Cookbooks

Dumplings may not rival Marie Antoinette's brioche as a globally renowned foodstuff but they are certainly well represented in historical records and cookbooks worldwide. This is not surprising, considering that it is a ubiquitous food, steeped in tradition. The evolution of the dumpling can be traced by comparing recipes from the yellowed pages of books of a bygone era with those from the glossy, colourful publications that fill the cookery sections of bookshops and the kitchen shelves of the middle classes. Many of the recipes collected in books from the nineteenth and twentieth centuries provide a record of how dumplings have been prepared and eaten for hundreds of years. Even now, the most traditional recipes are still used in modern kitchens and factories and are strictly adhered to, especially when celebratory meals are concerned. Many new varieties, resulting from experimentation in kitchens and restaurants, are influenced by the desire to fuse and combine different world cuisines and unusual ingredients to make everyday meals more interesting and appealing.

Wontons, Chinese dumplings made of very thin wrappers and often served in a broth. The etymology of the word could refer to their irregular shape.

Etymology

Despite copious references, the etymology of some of the words used to describe dumplings in different languages is not always clear. Through written or oral tradition several interpretations emerge, most of which link the origin of the different words either to their shape or to their filling. As is clear from the glossary at the end of this book, there are many names for dumplings, reflecting the fact that they can be compacted or folded into many different shapes and filled with various combinations of ingredients.

The English word 'dumpling', for example, has been traced back to the sixteenth or seventeenth century, when the now obsolete noun 'dump', which probably meant 'lump', was given a diminutive suffix. The more recent *cepelinai*, on the other hand, which became popular in Ukraine in the mid-twentieth century, derived its name from the German airship designed by Count Ferdinand von Zeppelin, because of its oblong shape and large size.

In Mandarin some dumplings are called *huntun*, which roughly means 'irregularly shaped', and are the equivalent of the Cantonese 'wonton', which means 'swallowing clouds' and could refer to the steam rising from the hot filling when the dumpling is bitten into or even to the irregular shape and white or translucent colour of some dumplings.

The etymology of *jiaozi* also has slightly different explanations, both of which relate to its shape. According to some, it was invented by Zhang Zhongjing (AD 150–220), a practitioner of traditional Chinese medicine and author of *Shang Han Za Bing Lun* (Treatise on Cold Pathogenic and Miscellaneous Diseases). Zhang was committed to helping Chinese people from all social classes fight disease, and developed a special soup made with mutton, peppers and medicinal ingredients to placate not just hunger but also cold and even frostbite afflicting the ears. The soup contained ear-shaped dumplings, the name of which, *jiaozi*, comes from the same root as the word for ear. A different interpretation has it that *jiaozi* derives its name from its horn shape, as the Chinese for horn is *jiao*, which signified the shape of gold ingots and was a symbol of wealth.

I encountered very similar difficulties when researching the origins of the Italian word 'ravioli'. According to different but equally reputable sources, the name derived from the verb *ravvolgere* (to wrap), the noun *rovogliolo* (knot) or the medieval Latin word *rabiola* (small turnip), all referring to the round shape of the pasta wrapped around the filling. The last suggestion is the one preferred by Giacomo Devoto, Italian linguist and president – between 1963 and 1972 – of the Accademia della Crusca, the institute for the protection and study of the Italian language. Other sources suggest that the name derives from *raviggiolo*, a cheese previously used in place of ricotta as a filling. In this case the name of the filling would eventually have come to describe any dumpling, regardless of its stuffing. This interpretation was favoured by Piero Camporesi, a professor at the University of Bologna between 1969 and 1996, and an expert in the social history of food and nutrition.

Another typically Italian linguistic controversy relates to the difference between Ligurian ravioli and Piedmontese *agnolotti*. The different names could refer to different fillings rather than to shapes, since green vegetables and cheese were staples of the Ligurian diet while meat and eggs were very prominent in the robust Piedmontese cooking. This interpretation is supported by the definitions of ravioli and *agnolotti* in the first dictionary of the Italian language, published in 1612 by the Accademia della Crusca. However, the origin of

The shape of Italian tortellini is thought to be inspired by Lucrezia Borgia's navel.

the name *agnolotti* could be either *agnello* (lamb), after the first meat filling used in Piedmont, or *anello* (ring), after the dumplings' original shape as a circle.

Whatever the origins of the words used in different languages, dumplings are named and sometimes pictured in those sources – which include commercial contracts, chronicles and letters – that historians use to increase their understanding of the society and traditions of the past.

Historical Records of Medieval Italian Dumplings

Medieval Italian dumplings, particularly, pop up in a number of historical documents that help to inform the debate about the origins and evolution of this prominent food through the everyday life of the so-called Dark Ages.

A visit to the chapel of Castel d'Appiano, near Bolzano in northern Italy, reveals a thirteenth-century fresco depicting the locally famous *mangiatrice di canederli* (dumpling eater), which provides the earliest available record of this typical south Tyrolean dish. The series of frescoes decorating the walls of the chapel represents the life of Christ and the Apostles in unmistakable Romanesque style, with a lack of perspective amply compensated for by vibrant colours and the familiarity of the depicted scenes. The Nativity scene consists of a typically two-dimensional representation of Mary and Joseph having a well-deserved rest while the Christ Child is asleep in the manger. Joseph sits at Mary's feet, resting his head on the palm of one hand and looking dreamy and contented. Mary lies on her side with her back to the crib and the stylized donkey and bull, turning her attention to a servant, the dumpling eater, who is cooking for the family. The servant, dressed

Thirteenth-century fresco in the chapel of Castel d'Appiano representing a servant making *canederli* in a large pan.

in a green robe and yellow hair covering, is squatting by a pan that is placed on a lively fire and is full to the brim with round, appetising dumplings. The servant is pictured in the act of tasting one of the dumplings by bringing it to her mouth using a large fork. The type of dumpling represented in the fresco is *canederli*, a large ball of dough made of stale bread and milk with the addition of bacon, beetroot, fresh cheese, spinach, mushrooms or even fruit, ricotta cheese and sugar, boiled in broth or water. *Canederli* is also popular in Germany, Austria and Switzerland, where it is called *Knödel* or *Klösse*. The visit to the chapel can be combined with a stop at the nearby tavern, which – in common with all the restaurants in the region – includes dumplings among the local specialities on its menu.

Ravioli is well-documented throughout the twelfth and thirteenth centuries, and the town of Gavi in Piedmont claims the honour of being its birthplace. (Gavi is not the only Italian

Pieter Bruegel the Elder, *The Land of Cockaigne*, 1567, oil on panel, from Boccaccio's *Decameron*. Cockaigne was a mythical land of plenty.

town to make this claim.) Members of the Raviolo family were said to have invented this dumpling and popularized it by selling it to merchants and travellers at their *locanda* (public house) in Gavi, on the way to the busy commercial port of Genoa. The only 'proof' for such a claim is the family's coat of arms, with its crude picture of a dumpling topped by three stars.

That the *raviolus* was eaten in Parma before the end of the thirteenth century is recorded by Fra Salimbene di Adam (1221–*c*. 1290), also known as Fra Salimbene of Parma, in his *Cronica*, an important source of information on the history and traditions of the time. The Italian friar and historian wrote that he had eaten '*raviolos sine crusta de pasta*' (ravioli without a pasta wrapping) during the celebrations of Santa Chiara, which have commemorated the saint every year on 11 August since her death in 1253. He also wrote that as ravioli in Parma were smaller than those in Genoa and other Italian towns, they were called *raviolén* (small ravioli). That probably later became *anolén*, and might explain the origin of the word *anolini*, which is used exclusively to describe filled dumplings from Parma and its surrounding region.

The topic of size is encapsulated in a comic poem in the Biblioteca Ambrosiana, Milan (S.Q.O.VIII, 38):

> A very gallant son was granted to the *raviolo* because of its good fortune, and that son is the *anolino*, a keen follower and lover of chicken broth. As for its appearance, it resembles its own father, it is cut in the same way but it has less body [referring to the thinner wrapper] and better brain [the meat filling]. But as it remained small, it ended up been called *anolino* [small dumpling].

Even Giovanni Boccaccio (1313–1375), a prominent figure in the history of Italian literature and considered to be one of the founders of Renaissance humanism, could not help mentioning ravioli in his most famous work, the *Decameron*, a medieval collection of 100 allegorical stories, narrated over ten days and ten nights by seven young women and three young men taking refuge from the Black Death epidemic in a villa outside Naples. Boccaccio mentions ravioli in one of the best-known of his tales (*Decameron* VIII, 3), in which Calandrino, a simple man who is the object of many practical jokes, is convinced by his friends of the existence of a magical stone, the *heliotropia*, that has the power of making the person who carries it invisible. Calandrino is persuaded by his friends that such a stone can be found in the *paese del Bengodi* (land of plenty, known in English as Cockaigne), a land where food is in abundance, the vineyards are tied to their supports with strings of sausages rather than rope, and there is a mountain of grated cheese on which 'there were people who did nothing other than prepare *maccheroni* and ravioli and cook them

Etching after Louis Philippe Boitard (active 1738–63) representing a dumpling seller crying 'diddle diddle diddle dumplens oh', from a late series of the *Cries of London*.

Diddle Diddle Diddle Dumplens ho.

in a capon broth'. Of course, the mountain is also blessed by the presence of a river of the best wine, without the hint of a drop of water in it.

Such an abundance and variety of references confirm that ravioli and other filled dumplings have been a staple of the Italian diet for many centuries, served, as is the case today, as a first-course alternative to the more internationally acclaimed spaghetti, lasagne and *maccheroni*.

Recipe Books

With the invention of the printing press and the improvement of education, literacy rates increased across Europe and later the USA from just a few per cent of the population in the Middle Ages to an average of more than 50 per cent in the nineteenth century. Books became more affordable, and recipe books started to become a must-have resource for the middle-class woman, who was often in charge of household management and budgeting. By the nineteenth century cookbooks had begun to move away from elaborate and expensive recipes to include ideas of how to feed families every day of the week, often suggesting monthly plans and providing tips on how to make staple and standard food more interesting and cost-effective. Dumplings, a popular, simple and inexpensive food, fitted well into this new approach.

British and North American cookbooks published between 1840 and 1970 include many recipes for the dumpling, which was described both in 1918 and 1940 as one of the 'foods that will win the war'. Dumplings were an affordable staple of cosy family meals, perhaps not exciting or exotic but certainly tasty, filling and comforting. For many, dumplings still carry memories of heavy lids lifted off even heavier cast-iron casserole dishes to reveal steaming cuts of meat covered in thick gravy and surrounded by floating dumplings; the contrast between the textures of tough, grisly meat and fluffy dumplings evoking memories of childhood and the experience of growing up.

In his book *The Oxford Companion to Food* (1999), the food historian and author Alan Davidson wrote:

> A dumpling is a food with few, indeed no, social pretensions, and of such simplicity that it may plausibly be

supposed to have evolved independently in the peasant cuisines of various parts of Europe and probably in other parts of the world too. Such cuisines feature soups and stews, in which vegetables may be enhanced by a little meat. Dumplings, added to the soup or stew, are still, as they were centuries ago, a simple and economical way of extending such dishes.

"THE ROSE SHALL CEASE TO BLOW _ THE WORLD SHALL CEASE TO MOVE . THE SEA SHALL CEASE TO FLOW . &_ OH, SHOULD'ENT I LIKE SOME OF THEM DUMPLINGS"

Satirical print *c.* 1839 of a ballad seller looking longingly at some dumplings in a shop window.

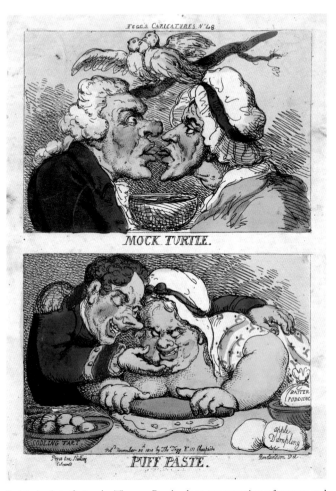

Satirical print of 1810 by Thomas Rowlandson, representing a footman and cook making puff pastry for apple dumplings.

The Department of Prints and Drawings of the British Museum in London has a number of eighteenth- and nineteenth-century prints that represent dumplings in scenes of everyday life. *Diddle diddle diddle dumplens ho*, for example, from

Hand-coloured portrait of the Duke of Norfolk caricatured as 'a Norfolk dumpling' by James Gillray, 1791.

the series 'The Cryes of the City of London Drawne after the Life' (1750–1821), shows a dumpling seller standing with a barrel under her left arm and a stick in her right hand, wearing a cape, apron and hat, her mouth open as she cries to attract the attention of passers-by. A lithograph from 1839 pictures a ballad seller looking longingly at dumplings stacked high on a plate visible in a shop window, and saying: 'The rose shall cease to blow . . . the world shall cease to move . . . the sea shall cease to flow . . . Oh should'ent I like some of them dumplings.'

The British Museum's twelve-volume *Catalogue of Political and Personal Satires* (1870–1954) contains a hand-coloured etching from 1810 by Thomas Rowlandson entitled *Puff Paste*, depicting two ugly figures, a hideous footman and a fat cook, caressing each other behind a table on which apple dumpling is being prepared, alongside codling tart and batter pudding tied in a bag. The catalogue also contains a series of satirical prints from 1791 by James Gillray, 'A Natural Crop alias a Norfolk Dumpling', depicting a rather plump duke of Norfolk wearing top-boots and a slouchy hat with closely cropped hair, holding the baton of the Earl Marshal.

The county of Norfolk was so closely associated with dumplings that 'Norfolk dumpling' became a term of mockery, as Gillray's prints demonstrate. The Norfolk dumpling, also known as a floater or floating dumpling, is the equivalent of the Yorkshire pudding. It is served with meat and was originally intended to disguise a small portion by providing a cheap and filling accompaniment. When resorts on the Norfolk coast became a popular destination for holidaymakers, dumplings were often on the menu of guest houses, as they provided filling meals at a relatively low cost. A Norfolk dumpling is light and fluffy; it floats to the surface of the broth or stew in which it is cooked, and contains no suet. *A Plain Cookery Book for the Working Classes* (1852) by Charles Elmé Francatelli, chief cook to Queen Victoria, contains many recipes for dumplings, including recipe no. 52, Norfolk dumplings, described as 'most excellent things to eke out an insufficient supply of baked meat for the dinner of a large family of children'.

As Francatelli's aim in writing this book was 'to show you how you may prepare and cook your daily food, so as to obtain from it the greatest amount of nourishment at the least possible expense', it is not surprising to find at least six recipes for dumplings, among them suet dumplings boiled with beef, rice dumplings, apple dumplings and yeast dumplings, which require the following ingredients: 'Two pounds of flour, a halfpenny worth of yeast, a pinch of salt, one pint of milk or water'. After being boiled for half an hour in a pot, not too fast, 'they must be eaten immediately, with a little butter or dripping, and salt or sugar.'

Dumplings were and still are popular in Suffolk, where no yeast or other raising agent is used in the mixture; in the Cotswolds, where suet, cheese and breadcrumbs are added; and in Scotland, where the traditional clootie dumpling is a steamed pudding with sultanas and other fruit served with custard.

In her *Book of Household Management* (1861), the Victorian writer Isabella Beeton includes advice on childcare, etiquette, entertaining and the employment of servants. Eight of her recipes are dedicated to savoury and sweet dumplings, including Sussex or hard dumplings, yeast dumplings and marrow dumplings, to be served in a soup, with meat or meat gravy; and boiled apple dumplings, currant dumplings and lemon dumplings, to be 'made into round balls' and dropped in boiling water or to be tied in cloth 'knitted in plain knitting, with very coarse cotton', boiled in water and then served as desserts with sifted sugar, cold butter or wine sauce. The recipes, which start with a list of ingredients (a feature that subsequently became the usual format for recipe books), are relatively easy to follow, and some have stood the test of time.

The popularity of dumplings in Victorian Britain, in particular Suffolk, is captured in Sheila Hardy's book *Arsenic in the Dumplings: A Casebook of Historic Poisonings in Suffolk* (2010), which describes how a chilling number of murders by arsenic poisoning were carried out by women using homemade food,

Floating dumplings are light and fluffy; they float to the surface of the broth or stew in which they are cooked and contain no suet.

including dumplings. Arsenic was widely and cheaply available from chemists until 1851, when the Sale of Arsenic Regulation Act introduced mandatory records of who purchased the poison, and also required colour to be added so that white arsenic powder could not be mistaken for or disguised as sugar or flour. The life-insurance business developed in the 1840s, and there were terrible cases of desperate parents poisoning their children in an attempt to support their families by supplementing their meagre income through insurance claims.

The English cook and television presenter Delia Smith has published many dumpling recipes throughout her long career, which began with her first cookery book in 1971. Still very popular throughout the 1970s, dumplings became less fashionable during the following three decades because of the increased availability and popularity of new varieties of rice, pasta and bread. However, contemporary British chefs seem to have rediscovered simple and hearty food, and have revisited traditional dumpling recipes and created interesting combinations for everybody to try in the kitchen. Jamie Oliver, for example, in his unmistakable style, named a recipe Tender-as-you-like Rabbit Stew with the Best Dumplings Ever, and included Asian Chicken with Coconut Dumplings in his fifteen-minute cookbook. Heston Blumenthal's Szechuan Broth with Duck Dumplings is hot and very tasty, as is Gary Rhodes's Curried Crab and Dumplings. Marco Pierre White suggests using brioche to make dumplings to serve with his Daube de Venison, while Rachel Khoo's ingredient for dumplings is baguette to accompany Boeuf Bourguignon. Gordon Ramsay and James Martin have produced the more traditional Chicken Casserole with Coriander Dumplings and Stew with Dumplings respectively. Nigella Lawson provides a recipe for Chicken Soup with Matzo Balls, and even explains how to extract schmaltz, or chicken fat, 'by plucking out the gobbets of chicken fat that cluster inside the cavity'.

Two well-known American dumpling recipes are chicken 'n' dumplings and boiled apple dumplings, the latter of which are nowadays considerably less popular than baked apple dumplings (not covered in this book). In the case of chicken 'n' dumplings, the size and texture of the flour-based dumplings can vary from small to large, and from firm to fluffy, depending on whether yeast has been used. The dumplings are cooked in boiling chicken broth with pieces of chicken and vegetables. The result is a thick, glutinous, comforting soup that is ideal for winter evenings.

In the *Hand-book of Practical Cookery, for Ladies and Professional Cooks: Containing the Whole Science and Art of Preparing Human Food* (1868), Pierre Blot, self-styled professor of gastronomy and founder of the New York Culinary Academy of Design, provides two recipes for boiled apple dumplings, one of which instructs the cook to

Quarter, peel and core the apples, and cut them in pieces, then envelope them in puff-paste [pastry] with beef-suet, boil till thoroughly done, and serve warm with sugar, or with apple or wine sauce. It may also be served with sauce for puddings.

The book also includes a recipe for plain fruit dumplings and explains how to make herb dumplings: 'Take a handful of the mildest herbs you can get, gather them so equal that the taste of one be not above the other, wash and chop them very small, put as many of them in as will make a deep green.'

Another classic American publication, *The White House Cook Book* (1887) by Mrs F. L. Gillette and Hugo Ziemann, steward of the White House, offers thirteen recipes for dumplings: egg dumplings for soup, suet dumplings for soup, dropped dumplings in lamb stew and in pork pot-pie, puff paste of suet 'excellent for fruit puddings and dumplings that are boiled', boiled apple dumplings, boiled rice dumplings with custard, two different recipes for suet dumplings, preserve dumplings, Oxford dumplings 'the size of an egg' and 'served with wine sauce', and lemon dumplings. In *Foods that Will Win the War and How to Cook Them* (1918), C. Houston Goudiss, food expert, and Alberta M. Goudiss, director of the School of Modern Cookery in New York, recommend dumplings as part of a filling family dinner menu, served with chicken fricassée, baked squash, peas, cranberry jelly, barley muffins and mock mince pie. They write: 'It would be well also to introduce dishes that extend the meat flavour, such as stews combined with dumplings, hominy [boiled corn kernels], or rice.'

Italian libraries are full to the brim with cookbooks, and two things are immediately clear from the very first glance at catalogues and indexes: dumpling recipes are not in short supply; and, as with many other Italian specialities, strong regional identities are captured in the many different names, shapes and ingredients.

To appreciate the degree of such regional differentiation, I feel the need to list some of the names I have come across in addition to the more common ravioli and tortellini: *agnolotti* (Piedmont), *cappelletti* (Modena), *pansotti* (Liguria), *caramelle* (Piacenza, in the shape of wrapped sweets), *anolini* (Parma), *agnoli* (Lombardy), *casoncelli* (Brescia), *marubini* (Cremona), *pegai* (Parma), *tordelli* (Lucca), *cappellacci* (Ferrara), *ravaiuoli* (Irpinia), *panzerotti* (Naples), *calzoncelli* (Puglia), *culingiones* or *cullurzones* (Sardinia), *cialzons* (Carnia) and also *fazzoletti*, *tortelli*, *tortelloni*, *fagotti* and *fagottini*. This impressive national list of dumplings can be matched only by the number of varieties present in different regions of China.

From the above list, the *agnolotto*, in both its meat and vegetable versions, features in the regional cookbook *La Cuciniera Piemontese* (The Cook from Piedmont) by an anonymous writer, published in Vercelli in 1771, and also in many

Freshly made Italian dumplings displayed in the window of a pasta shop.

recipes by Giovanni Vialardi, chef and patissier to the House of Savoy royal family in Italy between 1824 and 1853.

I will provide just a sample of the cookbooks that deal with dumplings. Alberto Consiglio wrote in *La Storia dei maccheroni* (1948) that 'Raviuoli were squares of thin dough that were filled with meat, salami or fresh cheese and, later on, sweet fillings.' In 1952 Ferruccio Botti, under the pseudonym Mastro Presciutto (Master Ham), collated many recipes typical of Parma in the *Gastronomia Parmense*. These included recipe no. 1, *Anolini*, which 'require a rather long preparation'; no. 3, *Anolini* 'light' with a filling of veal or chicken instead of beef, for 'people following special diets'; no. 4, *Pasticcio di anolini*, a pie with a filling of dumplings; no. 5.1, *Tortelli alle erbette*, with a filling of leafy vegetables; no. 5.2, *Tortelli alla Parmigiana*, with tomato sauce; no. 20, *Tortelli di zucca*, with a pumpkin filling; no. 21, *Tortelli di patate*, with potato filling; no. 59, *Tortelli dolci*, sweet dumplings; no. 114, *Tortellini di piccione*, filled with pigeon. All the recipes above are still in use, and it is customary to ask for a selection of fillings, for example a trio of meat, vegetables and cheese, when eating out in Italy.

No reference to Italian food would be complete without a look at what Pellegrino Artusi had to say in his *La Scienza in cucina e l'arte di mangiar bene* (Science in the Kitchen and the Art of Eating Well, 1891). The book, which is still widely available, was first published at the author's expense, but by the beginning of the twentieth century had become a best-seller found in all Italian kitchens. It is a collection of 790 recipes, including broths and soups, starters (entrées), main courses and desserts, and claims to be 'a practical manual that only requires the ability of holding a ladle'. All recipes are accompanied by anecdotes and personal remarks, and, for the first time in the history of Italian cookbooks, Artusi collated many regional expressions into a national gastronomical tradition.

African staples like yam and cassava are turned into dumplings and served with peanut soup.

Recipe no. 97 concerns 'naked' ravioli, also known in parts of the north of Italy as *malfatti* (badly shaped). These are made from a dough of ricotta cheese, spinach, egg, Parmesan cheese and nutmeg, shaped into small cylindrical dumplings, rolled in flour and cooked in boiling water. *Tortelli* also appear as recipe no. 55, and a note to an edition of 1970 reminds the reader that 'in the past the raviuolo could be with or without the pasta dough.'

There is even a recipe for ravioli by the famous Italian violinist and composer Niccolò Paganini dated 1840, the year he died. The recipe includes a flour-based dough without egg; a filling of beef, calf's brain, sausage, greens, egg and cheese; and a beef, mushroom and tomato sauce. Paganini had written about ravioli in a letter to his friend Luigi Germi in 1838: 'Every day, whether fasting or not, my mouth waters just at the thought of the delicious ravioli I have so often enjoyed at your table.'

It is very likely, then, that any Italian cookbook will include a few recipes for dumplings. However, that might not be the case in the future, as it is becoming less common to prepare dumplings from scratch in the home; most are now bought ready-made from specialist pasta shops and supermarkets.

Many contemporary African recipe books give an interesting modern take on traditional recipes from sub-Saharan Africa. Suggestions are offered as to different ingredients that allow shortcuts in preparation, to make it possible to reduce the hours, if not days, required to make certain foods, including dumplings, from scratch. I found recipes for many types of dumpling, reflecting the fact that, whether it is called *fufu*, *ugali*, *nzema*, *kenkey* or anything else, this is a staple of the African diet.

Dorinda Hafner covers a number of different types in her book *A Taste of Africa: With Over 100 Traditional African Recipes Adapted for the Modern Cook* (1993), and describes how dumplings should be served:

> Groundnut (Peanut) Soup with Fowl is usually served with Fufu, an Akan dumpling made from yams, cocoyams (taro), plantains, cassava or even processed potato flakes. The Fufu should sit like an island in a sea of soup, with the meat and fish scattered over the top.

The somewhat stodgy nature of African dumplings is also the subject of a popular Zimbabwean saying about the national dish, *sadza*: 'For *sadza* to enter [the body] it must be always supported by the sauce.'

Although questions remain about the etymology of the various names for dumplings around the world, the liveliness of the debate and the abundance of historical documents and essays about this food show just how important dumplings have been over the centuries in many different regional cuisines. Recipe books worldwide provide instructions and inspiration for preparing dumplings, which come very high on, and sometimes top of, the list of national dishes in a number of countries.

4
From Celebratory Feast to Street Food

The opening course of a traditional Christmas celebration meal in Poland is a steaming bowl of borscht with dumplings; the first course at most Italian Christmas meals is also homemade dumplings in a tasty, heart-warming broth covered in grated cheese. Dumplings also play a big role in many Jewish festivals, and are considered a 'good fortune food', to be eaten to celebrate Chinese New Year. With the transition from hand- to factory-made, dumplings have become a simple, ready-to-cook option for many busy working families and single people across the globe. This chapter looks at how dumplings are prepared and served as part of special celebrations, and also explores the role of this food as an everyday staple available in school and workers' canteens and sold in the street by vendors of countless nationalities.

Celebration Food

When travelling across the Mongolian steppes and accepting the hospitality of a nomadic family or visiting a home in the Buryatia region of Russia, the guest is offered hot tea and dairy products, with a plateful of steaming dumplings. As part of my research for this book, I boarded the Trans-Siberian Express train and stopped at Irkutsk, from where I made the short journey by bus to the historical town of Listvyanka on the shores of Lake Baikal. I spent a few days with a family of fishermen and enjoyed long walks in the woods while watching out for brown bears.

One evening I was invited to the home of an elder in the village and treated to the local traditional ceremony reserved for guests. The wooden house was warm and welcoming, with plenty of colourful rugs and cushions. The simple wooden table was covered with a white tablecloth and the opening courses were all white (fresh sliced cheese, cottage cheese, onions and rice cooked in milk), following a tradition going back to shamanic rituals. I was then served elaborately pleated dumplings with a steaming round opening at the top, filled with juicy minced yak meat seasoned with large amounts of black pepper. Making these dumplings is not easy. Pieces of dough are rolled one by one into small circles before the cook skilfully pinches and seals the edges into a round shape around the filling, leaving an open hole at the top through which steam escapes. The meal also included dishes of smoked fish, salad and pickled vegetables. At the end a choir of women wearing the traditional colourful dresses and tall, golden, tinkling headdresses joined the party, singing traditional folk-songs and reciting poems about the forces of nature and the power of love.

In Mongolian cuisine, which is very similar to Buryatian, the three types of dumpling are named according to the cooking method: *buuz* is steamed; *bansh* is boiled; and *khuushuur* is pan-fried. Although these are all served in most cafes and cheap eateries in the capital, Ulan Bator, they are also eaten on Tsagaan Sar, the Mongolian and Buryat New Year. In rural areas they are prepared in large batches and stored frozen outdoors ready

Steaming Chinese *baozi* from a street vendor.

to be dropped into a pan of boiling water at mealtimes or when a guest – expected or unexpected – arrives.

During Polish Christmas celebrations, dumplings are served before the customary main dish of carp. The Wigilia (Christmas Eve) meal is a vegetarian affair. The table is decorated with straw or hay, as a reminder of Baby Jesus' manger, and a blessed Holy Communion wafer, *oplatki*, is placed on a fine china plate. An extra place is set to accommodate any stranger who might happen to pass by. As darkness sets in, candles are lit, and after the wafer is broken and shared the dinner begins. A typical meal used to comprise thirteen main dishes, representing Christ and the twelve Apostles, and foods come from the forest (mushroom), the fields (grains), the orchard (fruit) and the sea or lakes (fish). Typical dishes now include borscht with small dumplings (*uszka*); carp in aspic; herring; breaded fish; cabbage; and larger dumplings (*pierogi*), all followed by a large number of desserts, such as fruit compote, nuts, poppy-seed rolls and gingerbread.

Similar Christmas celebrations take place in Russia and Ukraine. Homemade dumplings, *pelmeni* and *varenyky* respectively, are served in a broth before a large variety of other festive dishes is brought out.

Christmas Eve is the setting of one of Nikolai Gogol's stories first published in 1831–2 as part of the collection entitled *Evenings on a Farm near Dikanka*. In 'The Night before Christmas', a blacksmith named Vakula braves the elements and the darkness to meet his beloved Oksana. According to Russian folklore, the night before Christmas is a dangerous time when spirits, witches and ghosts are free to roam and wreak havoc. A series of events orchestrated by the Devil, who is irate with Vakula for painting hideous images of him in the local church, brings Vakula across the path of the mighty Cossack Puzaty Patsyuk. The scene of the encounter

Russian *pelmeni* served with borscht (beetroot soup) and pickled gherkins, a traditional meal served in Eastern Europe.

Tortellini in a broth is the first course in a traditional Italian Christmas meal.

features a plateful of magical *varenyky* flying through the air, plunging into a bowl of cream and then flying straight into the hungry, moustachioed mouth of Puzaty Patsyuk. The setting, in the depth of a thick forest in the middle of a snowstorm, is an accurate description of rural Russia in winter, as is the food described in the stories, which – in addition to the magical *varenyky* – include Cossack potatoes, Ukrainian borscht served with bread and sour cream, and pancakes with honey. Although many of the old beliefs have now ceased to exist, some traditions remain, for example that of serving filled dumplings with borscht, stuffed cabbage and wheat pudding on Christmas Eve.

In Italy, the main Christmas meal is enjoyed either on the evening of 24 December or at noon on the following day. After the family has returned from mass and the presents have been exchanged under the Christmas tree or by the Nativity scene, it is time to sit at the table to spend a few hours eating, talking and being merry. Starters often include homemade pickled vegetables and a selection of salami, ham and other cured meats. Tortellini or ravioli is served in a broth as the first course, followed by roast veal, stuffed poultry or fish, with plenty of vegetables. The dessert varies depending on the region; panettone and cream are probably the most popular. Dumplings for the Christmas meal are prepared by the women in the family over the two days preceding the festivities. Another traditional occasion on which to enjoy homemade dumplings is All Saints' Day, 1 November, when families get together after a visit to the cemetery to eat, talk and remember the dead.

In the homes of many Ashkenazi Jews across France, Germany, Russia and Eastern Europe, *knaidl* are a Passover speciality, while *kreplach* filled with minced meat or mashed potatoes is traditionally served at the last meal before the fast of Yom Kippur, on the seventh day of Sukkot (Hoshanah

Fresh wonton wrappers are now widely available in Asian supermarkets around the world.

Rabbah), on Purim and on other Jewish holidays. Claudia Roden includes Ashkenazi recipes in her *Book of Jewish Food*, such as *kreplach* with meat or chicken, 'sometimes served as a pasta first course with meat gravy from a roast'; and cheese *kreplach*, 'which are served as a starter or main dish in dairy meals'. The same book also includes recipes for fruit *varenikes*, also described as plum and apricot ravioli, which are 'best in a dairy meal, so that they can be served with sour cream or butter'. Among the Sephardic recipes, Roden includes pumpkin ravioli. She notes that the pumpkin has been associated with Jews since its arrival in Italy from the New World, because they were already familiar with it through their Spanish and Portuguese connections. Recipes for *rishta wa calsones* (tagliatelle and large ravioli filled with cheese) were probably taken to Syria and Egypt by Italian Jews at the beginning of the

Wontons in a broth – it is a Chinese belief that eating dumplings on New Year's Eve brings good luck.

sixteenth century, when a mass migration to the east followed the expulsion of Jews from Southern Europe.

In southwestern Germany *Maultaschen* (literally 'mouth pockets') were traditionally reserved for the days leading up to Easter, although they are now available throughout the year ready-made in many shops. They are similar to Italian ravioli but bigger, with a filling of minced meat, spinach, breadcrumbs, onions and spices, and are said to have been invented by monks to conceal the fact that meat was eaten during Lent. Their alternative name, *Herrgottsbescheisserle*, means 'little ones who cheat the Lord'.

Of all traditional Chinese festivals, the celebrations for the arrival of the New Year are some of the most colourful and elaborate. As in many other cultures, a festival like this is a time for families and friends to get together, reflect on the past and plan for the future. The date varies every year, as the celebrations must fall on the first day of the first moon of the lunar calendar. Preparations start well in advance with the cleaning of the house and the putting up of decorations, including scrolls carrying messages of good luck and images of symbolic fruit and flowers. The Kitchen God is bid farewell a few days before the end of the year, when it leaves the house to report to other gods on the behaviour of the household during the year. All foods, including homemade dumplings, have to be prepared before New Year's Day, when families get together and children are given red envelopes with money for good luck. The end of the holidays is marked, after about two weeks, by a festival of lanterns and a parade led by a dancing dragon.

Some say that eating *jiaozi* as part of the Chinese New Year celebrations 'will keep wealth in the family as the dough keeps the filling from escaping'. For this reason, dumplings are served at weddings and other celebrations, and it is considered by some that breaking the wrapper of a dumpling while lifting it out of the cooking liquid will bring bad luck.

Another reason for the association of *jiaozi* with good luck is probably its shape, which is reminiscent of ingots of gold or silver as they were shaped in ancient China. In the folktale 'The Magical Dumplings' as told by Katherine Liang Chew in 2008, the grandmother (Nainai in Mandarin) says, while making dumplings for the New Year celebrations in the kitchen: 'The shape and colour of a dumpling looks like a Ding of silver, a silver ingot. Eating dumplings carries with it the New Year wish of prosperity.' Rows of snow-white dumplings, just enough to feed the poor family of the grandfather (Yeye in Mandarin) and grandmother, are lined up on a tray, ready for the cooking pot, when a half-frozen old man with a white

Hanami dango, colourful sweet dumplings on a skewer, served with tea in Japan.

Sakura dumplings are eaten in Japan as part of the celebrations for the arrival of spring.

beard appears out of nowhere and is invited to share the meal. As is Chinese tradition, the guest is asked to help himself from the communal bowl; to the astonishment and desperation of the hungry family, he finishes all the dumplings and asks for more. When he is given the few remaining dumplings, he starts serving the rest of the family and by magic produces a very large quantity of food, which is more than enough to satisfy everybody's appetite. He then disappears mysteriously into the snow, leaving behind fox footprints. It becomes clear that the family has received the visit of the Fox Fairy, disguised as a needy old man bringing the family good fortune for the New Year.

Hanami is the Japanese tradition of 'enjoying the beauty of flowers'. It is such an important pastime that blossom forecasts are produced daily at the beginning of the spring to help plan for *sakura*, or cherry-blossom season. The first *hanami* festivals were celebrated by Japanese aristocrats in the eighteenth century, but it gradually became a pastime for all classes. *Sakura* walks have been the inspiration for many haiku, and *sakura* picnics, set under the best white or pink blossoming trees, are colourful and enjoyable. The Japanese proverb '*Hana yori dango*' (dumplings over flowers) suggests that for some cherry-blossom viewers food is more important than the beauty of the blooms. *Hanami dango* – a dish consisting of three dumplings on a skewer, one pink, one white and one green – is eaten during cherry-blossom season. Japanese sweet dumplings can be served on their own or with *anko* (red-bean paste) or *goma* (black sesame paste), while savoury varieties are served with soy-based sauce and nori seaweed sprinkled on top.

Staple Food, Street Food and the Ready-to-cook Market

Dumplings are a convenient and filling staple, and make the perfect street food because once prepared they are very quick to cook and assemble and can be eaten on the go. During my Siberian travels I found tasty *pelmeni*, a Russian national dish, in typical workers' restaurants (*stolovaya*) across the country, alongside borscht, *kasha* (porridge), stuffed cabbage and pickled vegetables. In Yekaterinburg, a major city east of the Ural Mountains on the border of Europe and Asia, between exploring the nearby forests and historical sites (the city is the unfortunate place where the last tzar and his family met their untimely and rather grim death), I had a taste of the traditional Ural recipe that requires a mixture of 45 per cent beef, 35 per cent mutton and 20 per cent pork.

In Warsaw and Krakow, and undoubtedly many other Polish towns, *pierogi* can be enjoyed in a *bar mleczny* (milk bar), cafeterias that were once subsidized by the government, or bought from the kiosks and hole-in-the-wall-type shops that now compete in town centres with American fast-food outlets and Turkish kebab shops. *Pierogi* are bought by the number and dropped, still frozen, into boiling water. They are ready in minutes and served on a Styrofoam tray with the condiment of choice. Although they are clearly not a Michelin-star experience, I always find the chunky and slightly chewy dough and the juicy filling satisfying.

When travelling in Japan, I discovered that dumplings are on the menu at most noodle bars, where at least a couple of pictures of *yaki-gyoza* or similar can be spotted among numerous photos of noodle soups and other noodle-based dishes on the front of vending machines. The vending-machine experience can be very confusing for the first-time foreign

Filling dumplings with sweet red bean paste.

Japanese *gyoza* and *nikuman* plastic food models on display in a restaurant in Osaka, Japan.

Vending machine in a noodle bar in Japan.

customer without a grasp of the Japanese language, but it is definitely a skill worth acquiring, in particular in large cities. The customer of a noodle bar, for example, is required to purchase a ticket from a vending machine at the entrance before sitting at a table where a waiter will exchange the ticket for the paid-for meal without having to handle cash. The most popular varieties of Japanese dumpling are *gyoza,* which is very similar to Chinese *jiaozi*; *yaki-gyoza,* similar to Chinese *guotie*; and *nikuman,* equivalent to the Chinese *baozi* and mostly sold as a street food at busy stations and junctions.

Another street food sold at busy junctions is the Latin American *tamales.* Cooked in *tamaleras* (giant steamers) set up at street corners, they are eaten on the go after peeling off the banana-leaf wrapper or taken home for a family ready-meal.

Most dumplings are now readily available in cans or vacuum-packed containers or frozen in large bags from supermarkets all over the world. Wonton wrappers for Chinese dumplings can be made at home from fresh dough, but they can also be bought in large blocks of pre-made individual wrappers, with cornflour (cornstarch) dusted in between to keep them from sticking together. Ready-made wontons and *baozi* are also available, fresh or frozen, and can be cooked in a few minutes in a traditional steamer or in the microwave. Industrially made ravioli are available refrigerated, with a shelf life of a few weeks; dried, in plastic bags, with a shelf life of a few months; or canned, usually in tomato sauce, with a shelf life of many months. Refrigerated or dried ravioli can be of very good quality, but more elaborate and creative fillings can be found only in specialist shops or made at home. In Russia, shop-bought *pelmeni* are associated with the student or bachelor lifestyle, much as instant noodles are in the West.

Tinned ravioli has been in the supermarkets since the 1970s.

Dim sum treat with pumpkin and red bean paste.

Dim Sum Menu

Beef Ball Dumplings Steamed seasoned minced beef
in tofu wrappers

Cha Siu Bao Steamed buns stuffed with barbecued pork

Cheung Fun Rice-noodle sheets filled with shrimp,
beef and pork and steamed

Curried Squid Dumplings Squid marinated in a curry sauce
and steamed

Crescent Dumplings (Ham Sui Gok) Steamed glutinous (sweet)
pastry filled with pork, shrimp and mushroom

Egg Custard Buns Steamed buns filled with savoury custard
and meat or seafood

Fun Gor Translucent dumplings filled with pork
and bamboo shoots

Har Gau Shiny, translucent shrimp dumplings

Jiaozi Meat-filled parcels of dough boiled in water

Lo Bak Goh Steamed cake made with Chinese turnip and rice flour

Lo Mai Gai Sticky rice, chicken and sausage meat wrapped in
lotus leaves and steamed

Sesame Seed Dumplings Balls of glutinous rice flour and brown sugar
filled with sweet red-bean paste, rolled in sesame seeds and steamed

Spring Rolls Made with a thin wrapper. Lighter and less filling
than egg rolls, filled with dried mushrooms, shredded meat
and carrot or bamboo shoots, and seasoned with oyster sauce,
soy sauce and sugar

Siu Mai Steamed dumplings shaped like a basket with a filling
of shrimp, pork and crab, sprinkled with fish roe

Taro Dumplings Pan-fried dumplings with a wrapper made from
mashed taro root and filled with pork, dried shrimp,
and Chinese dried mushrooms

Egg Custard Tart Baked puff pastry filled with egg custard

Mango Pudding Silky blend of fresh mango and cream

Sweet Cream Buns Steamed buns filled with egg custard

A Chinese Tradition: Dim Sum

Teahouses across China must have been very popular among travellers making their way up and down the Silk Road, and farmers in need of refreshment and relaxation after a long day in the fields. Dim sum, which can be variously translated as 'heart warmers', 'heart's delights' or 'to touch your heart', is a Chinese eating custom originally from Canton, where customers were served snacks to nibble while sipping tea. Nowadays, dim sum consists of a variety of dumplings made of flour-based edible wrappers or inedible wrappers made of lotus or banana leaves, served in small portions and usually in the bamboo baskets in which they have been steamed, to keep them warm. Lighter, steamed dishes are served first, followed by fried dishes and finally dessert. In traditional restaurants the food is wheeled around on trolleys, but it is more and more common to order by ticking a number of options on an incredibly long menu. In X'ian, a city in the north of China, dim sum dinners or 'dumpling banquets' are actively promoted by the local tourist board and travel agents as a must-do experience. The tastes, colours and shapes of the dumplings, many of which are inspired by unusual stories, deeply rooted in local culture, are combined to create spectacular displays.

5

Folklore, Literature and Film

A staple food the world over and a national dish in many countries, the dumpling appears as a prop, an extra or even a character in works of literature, folkloric tales, poetry, film, songs and nursery rhymes. A few monuments and gastronomic or historical societies are devoted to raising the profile and protecting the history and heritage of very specific types of dumpling in countries as diverse as Italy, Ukraine and the USA. This chapter celebrates the dumpling in its artistic and quirky representations, and is intended as a collection of curious examples of how a simple food can be so deeply rooted in society and come to embody everything that is traditional, familiar and comforting.

Across Central Asia and the Middle East, Mullah Nasreddin or Hodja Nasrudin is a well-known folkloric and satirical character, a 'wise fool' whose adventures are captured in timeless, brief, meaningful tales that deliver moral lessons through subtle humour. Since the thirteenth century, generation after generation, Nasreddin's tales have been narrated and added to, and they provide an accurate depiction of everyday life in small villages. The character's passion for dumplings, and the misunderstanding that followed, are the subject of an Uzbek tale, which recounts that one day Nasreddin was travelling on

Bronze statue of Mullah Nasreddin, a famous character of many Central Asian folkloric tales, in Bukhara, Uzbekistan.

his donkey and decided to stop for lunch at the house of a friend whose small dumplings (*chuchvara*) were renowned all over town. Nasreddin was in luck: the cook had made fresh *chuchvara* that very morning and they were hanging from the branches of a small tree near the kitchen, where they had been placed to dry in the sun. Lunch was served and Nasreddin could not stop praising the delicious *chuchvara* he had just been given. As he was leaving the house, still praising the cook for the delicious meal, he noticed the tree by the kitchen and, thinking the dumplings were growing from its branches, asked his host if he would be so kind as to give him a cutting to take home. The host, although baffled by the unusual request, cut

Popular Japanese folkloric hero Momotaro with his travel companions:
'Momotaro, Momotaro please give me one of your dumplings.'

a small branch and gave it to Nasreddin, who is still patiently watering the plant and wondering why dumplings are not growing on it.

As Mullah Nasreddin and his adventures are popular in Central Asia and the Middle East, so is Momotaro in Japan, and it is significant, in the context of the dumpling's role as a comforting everyday staple, that he is also very fond of dumplings. Momotaro's tale, a true classic in Japanese storytelling, tells of an old man and his wife who could not have children. One day they found a giant peach in a field and, to their great surprise, discovered a baby inside it. The baby grew to be a big boy, and it was not long before he was ready to leave his home and go off to fight the demons that were troubling the local community. His parents helped him to prepare for the journey, made him a bag of dumplings and saw him off. The version by Sayumi Kawauchi, translated by Ralph F. McCarthy and published in the book *Once Upon a Time in Japan* (1985), continues:

> Smiling and waving, [Momotaro] marched straight off to Demon's Island with the bag of dumplings hanging from his belt. On the way he met a dog. 'Momotaro, Momotaro, please give me one of your dumplings. If you do, I'll go with you and help you fight the demons,' barked the dog. So Momotaro gave him a dumpling and set off again with the dog close behind him. Before they had gone far they met a monkey and a pheasant. And for the price of one dumpling each, these two also agreed to accompany Momotaro.

With the help of his companions, big and strong Momotaro fought the demons and earned their respect and the gratitude of all villagers who held him as a hero. Momotaro's ability to engage the support of his travel companions and to fight the demons successfully would not have been quite the same without his bag of dumplings, which represents, in its simplicity, the strength he derived from his loving family.

Rice dumplings feature with traditional folkloric characters in 'The Old Woman who Lost her Dumpling' (1902), one of the many tales published by Patrick Lafcadio Hearn (1850–1904) as part of his collection entitled *Japanese Fairy Tales* (1918). The tale is about a woman who, while making rice-flour dumplings, dropped one, which rolled into a hole in the floor. As she was trying to reach it, she fell down the hole after it and found herself in a different country where there lived a terrifying Oni, a gigantic people-eating demon. The woman kept following her rolling dumpling and was captured by the Oni. As she was good at making dumplings, she was spared a sorrowful end and given a job in the kitchen instead. After a few adventures at the service of the Oni, the woman eventually managed to escape and return home with a magic rice paddle that allowed her to produce an infinite amount of dumplings and become very rich.

This strong link between dumplings and tradition was used by the Japanese writer Sōseki Natsume to represent the contradictions of Japanese society during the revolutionary Meiji era, a period during which Japan and its traditions start-ed, for the first time in history, to emerge from isolation and merge with Western culture. In his novel *I Am a Cat* (1906), Sōseki describes upper-middle-class characters making fools of themselves by trying too hard to imitate Western customs. Many aspects of their everyday life are still strongly rooted in the centuries-old Japanese tradition, for example the way they dress, the etiquette that rules interpersonal relationships and, of course, the food they eat. In an amusing passage from the translation by Aiko Ito and Graeme Wilson from 1972, Waverhouse, the talkative and self-centred friend of Mr Sneaze, tries to persuade him and his wife to enjoy some simple and thoroughly Japanese dumplings:

> Let's go try some of Imozaka's famous dumplings. Have you ever tried those dumplings? You, too, Mrs Sneaze, sometime you really ought, if only just once, to try them. They're beautifully soft and even more beautifully cheap.

Waverhouse's suggestion clearly goes against the enormous efforts of pompous Mr Sneaze and his snooty wife to dis-tance themselves from Japanese traditions. Instead, they try to 'better' themselves by embracing everything that comes from the West and turning up their noses at anything associated with Japanese tradition.

Japanese *nikuman* filled with eels, steamed in bamboo baskets, a speciality of Miyajima island in Japan.

In the same way as the changes in the Meiji era threatened traditions in Japan, including foods with strong associations with the past, in Italy, Filippo Tommaso Marinetti, founder of the Futurist movement in art and a supporter of Fascism, provoked all Italians in 1931 by calling for the abolition of pasta in his Manifesto of Futurist Cuisine. The manifesto stated:

> We believe in the abolition of pasta, the absurd Italian gastronomic religion. Maybe the English derive strength from their cod, roast beef and pudding, the Dutch from their meat and cheese, the Germans from their sauerkraut, smoked bacon and sausage; but the Italians do not derive strength from pasta.

The main motivation for this message was political: the regime needed to reduce the demand for pasta to address the shortages and price increases of wheat, which was largely imported. Marinetti said that 'one thinks, dreams and acts according to what one eats and drinks', and questioned the nutritional value of pasta, accusing it of causing a series of weaknesses in the Italian population including 'scepticism, sentimentalism, tiredness, pessimism, nostalgic inactivity and neutrality'. However, a group of artists from Genoa came out in support of the local speciality, ravioli, and wrote to Marinetti saying that they supported the stance taken against 'macaroni, vermicelli, spaghetti and tortellini' but asked for a declaration of 'sincere neutrality toward the ravioli, optimistic and dynamic engines for which we have deep sympathy and a duty of gratitude and friendship'. Apparently Marinetti received poetical declarations of support for ravioli from other Futurist artists, including the painter Vittorio Osvaldo Tommasini (known as Farfa), who saw ravioli, probably because of its shape, as a 'meaty love letter'.

Ho Xuan Huong, a Vietnamese concubine at the turn of the nineteenth century, wrote witty and erotic poems, often addressing women's oppression in a patriarchal society. The beautiful poem reproduced below, which appeared in *Poetry* magazine in April 2008 translated by Marilyn Chin, contains a typical symbol of Chinese and Asian poetry, a ripe fruit or dumpling that represents the body of a woman.

> Floating sweet dumpling
> My body is powdery white and round
> I sink and bob like a mountain in a pond
> The hand that kneads me is hard and rough
> You can't destroy my true red heart.

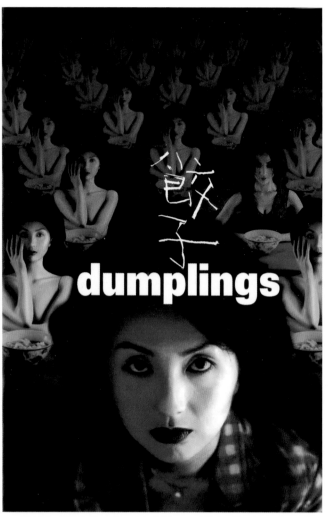

Dumplings (2004) film poster.

Film

In the Far East, dumplings, because of their ubiquitous status as an everyday food, are the subject of beautiful or significant scenes in a variety of films. The opening of *Eat Drink Man Woman* (1994), an internationally acclaimed film by the Taiwanese director Ang Lee, shows dumplings being prepared as part of the sumptuous and very traditional banquet that Mr Chu, a chef, widower and father of three grown-up daughters, prepares every Sunday for his family. It is at the table that the tension between tradition and modernity surfaces and is addressed through a sequence of announcements and surprises.

The film *Gaau Ji* (*Dumplings*, 2004), by the Hong Kong director Fruit Chan, contains a long and suggestive close-up scene about making dumplings. The story concerns a neglected wife who is prepared to do anything to stay young and attractive, including eating wontons filled with a special and extremely gruesome ingredient. The secret recipe has been developed by a former gynaecologist who performed illegal abortions before turning to the lucrative but no less disturbing business of helping rich women to mask their age.

In the film *Oldboy* (2003) by the South Korean director Park Chan-Wook, based on a Japanese manga, the main character is kidnapped and locked for fifteen years in a room in a secret location. Every meal he is given consists of dumplings (Korean *gunmandu*) from a nearby restaurant. When he is mysteriously released, he uses his memory of the dumpling's taste to track down the person who imprisoned him. He goes from restaurant to restaurant until he recognizes the taste of the dumpling he had been fed throughout his imprisonment, and in the end manages to carry out his ferocious revenge.

Oldboy (2003) film poster.

Advert for Taiwanese film *Eat Drink Man Woman* (1994).

The popular animated film *Kung Fu Panda* (2008) contains entertaining scenes that revolve around dumplings. The main character is Po, a clumsy, dumpling-loving panda who aspires to become a kung fu master under the guidance and strict training of Master Shifu. Po's lack of skill in kung fu seems insurmountable until Shifu discovers that Po is capable of incredible physical challenges when motivated by food. The scene of the Battle of the Dumpling between Po and Shifu is particularly action-packed and memorable.

In the sequel, *Kung Fu Panda 2* (2011), Po's appetite for dumpling has not diminished and there is a hilarious scene where Po the Dumpling Warrior tries to impress his five masters by stuffing his mouth with no fewer than 40 dumplings. The contest ends in disaster, however, when a congratulatory pat on the back from Master Crane causes Po to spit them all out.

Children's Characters

Cute cartoon characters and animations inspired by dumplings are popular in East Asia, where they appear in comics, cartoons, video games and soft toys. In the West, meanwhile, references to the dumpling can be spotted in children's books and songs, including a number of traditional nursery rhymes.

Michael Bond's Paddington Bear, for example, has a humorous adventure involving a scary giant dumpling in the story 'Something Nasty in the Kitchen' from *Paddington Helps Out* (first published in 1960). Mr and Mrs Brown are in bed with flu and Mrs Bird, the housekeeper at 32 Windsor Gardens, is away. Paddington decides to take charge of the kitchen and prepare a meal for his family, but things do not quite go to plan. He starts by boiling the cabbage in the kettle and using the water to make an undrinkable coffee for Mr Brown. Then,

Giant panda Po eating dumplings in the film *Kung Fu Panda* (2008).

as 'Paddington was very keen on stew, especially when it was served with dumplings', he proceeds to make a dumpling mixture inside his hat, as he has run out of bowls. Once in the boiling water, the dumpling mixture gets out of control. It pushes up the lid of the pan and starts hanging over the side of the stove like a shapeless monster. At this stage, a fretful Paddington loses his cool, places his hat on his head a bit too firmly and runs for the door. 'I am afraid I can't raise my hat because it is stuck down with dumpling mixture', he tells his friend Mr Gruber, who has arrived just in time to rescue the situation and help him tidy up the kitchen before Mrs Bird returns. The story, in common with all Paddington's other adventures, has a happy ending.

Since many nursery rhymes and children's songs are about food, including cakes, potatoes, porridge, sausages and hot cross buns, it is not surprising that a few are centred on the dumpling. 'Diddle Diddle Dumpling', a traditional street cry of dumpling sellers, has for at least two centuries featured as a line in a popular nursery rhyme, which is now – because of its strong rhythm – part of a selected core of poetry recommended for Year 1 children (aged five to six) in the UK:

Diddle diddle dumpling
My son John
Went to bed
With his trousers on
One shoe off
And one shoe on
Diddle diddle dumpling
My son John.

'Diddle Diddle Dumpling' and 'Pussycat Ate the Dumplings' are two of the hundreds of rhymes collated in *The Real Mother Goose* (first published in 1916), a very successful children's book with distinctive pen and watercolour illustrations by Blanche Fisher Wright.

Pussycat ate the dumplings, the dumplings
Pussycat ate the dumplings
Mama stood by, and cried, 'oh, fie!
Why did you eat the dumplings?'

'Davy Davy Dumpling' is often used in parents' and babies' groups as a 'tickle' rhyme, where parents are encouraged to change the first line by swapping 'Davy' for their baby's name and to wiggle, tickle and nibble the baby, mimicking the content of the following lines:

Davy Davy Dumpling
Boil him in a pot
Sugar him, and butter him
And eat him while he's hot!

Song

The song 'Il Tortellino', presented during the 51st Zecchino d'Oro (2008), a televised Italian singing competition for children, describes a mother's struggle to get her fussy little boy to eat his food. After spending fruitless hours in the kitchen preparing the most delicious and elaborate recipes, she decides to summon a council of other mothers to try and find a solution. After long deliberations it is decided to try tortellini, the ring-shaped filled dumpling originally from Bologna. The plan is successful and the choir happily sings:

> It is the tortellino from Bologna
> With broth without cream
> Mum's secret
> To clean the plate
> From that day in the homes
> When it is dinner time
> Children with their finger
> are measuring
> That ancient and funny ring
> In the shape of a belly-button.

Dumplings even made it into 'The Dumpling Song' by the UK pop group Pet Shop Boys; that song also features in David Almond's play for the under-tens *My Dad's a Birdman*, about Lizzie Crow and her dad Jack who are trying to cope with Lizzie's mother's death with the help of Auntie Doreen's comforting dumplings and a no-nonsense approach to life.

Dumplings are not just celebrated in nursery rhymes and children's songs. A well-known Cuban song from the 1950s, 'Los Tamalitos de Olga', celebrates the delicious *tamales* sold by a street vendor in Cienfuegos.

Festivals and Events

A very different aspect of cultural heritage is linked to the role of food festivals in celebrating traditions characteristic of a region, town or community. As we have seen, the dumpling has played a very important part in food history and tradition, and so it is not surprising to find festivals focusing on dumplings – some of them rather curious.

The Rice Dumpling Festival, also known as the Dragon Boat Festival, falls on the fifth day of the fifth month of the Chinese lunar calendar, and is widely celebrated in China. The festival commemorates Qu Yuan, a patriotic poet who threw himself into the Ni Lo river in 278 BC when his land was captured by enemies. During the celebrations, Chinese people throw rice dumplings into the river as offerings to Qu Yuan, and play drums and gongs to frighten away fish and other sea creatures to prevent them from attacking Qu Yuan's body. Rice dumplings are prepared by families before the celebration

Dumpling-making competition in Shenyang, China.

Oliver Onion, Cheese Chester and Pirate Parrot taking part in the Great Pierogi Race during the interval of a Pittsburgh Pirates match in Pennsylvania, U.S.

and are given as gifts to relatives and friends or presented as offerings to the ancestors.

More than 100 contestants take part annually in a dumpling-making competition in Shenyang, the capital of northeast China's Liaoning province. The dumplings are judged on their quality and quantity, and after the competition they are donated to local retirement homes and migrant workers.

In the U.S. state of Pennsylvania, the unusual Great Pittsburgh Pierogi Race N'at is a race between baseball mascots that takes place during Pittsburgh Pirates games. Four contestants race in giant dumpling (Polish *pierogi*) costumes: Jalapeño Hannah in a green hat, Cheese Chester in yellow, Sauerkraut Saul in red and Oliver Onion in purple, with Potato Pete, in blue, making occasional appearances. The dumplings usually run around the track and at times they are distracted or knocked to the ground by intruder mascot Pirate Parrot. Once a year the racing dumplings team takes on the Milwaukee Brewers' racing sausages and, separately, the Washington Nationals' racing U.S. Presidents.

Polish dumplings are also celebrated, together with other Polish traditions, in the annual Pierogi Fest in Whiting, Indiana.

Pierogi Festival logo – this festival is organized by descendants of Polish immigrants in the town of Whiting, Indiana.

Food festivals themed around ravioli are very popular throughout Italy and combine the opportunity to taste local specialities with live music and dance.

The festival is organized by descendants of Polish immigrants, to celebrate their ethnic heritage by reproducing, in a humorous way, some of their family memories. During the three-day festival, locals dressed as dumplings take part in and host singing and dancing competitions as well as a Pierogi Toss event, in which dumplings have to be thrown backwards and over the head, and a Pierogi Eating contest, which consists of three minutes to stuff one's mouth with dumplings. The costumes include the popular Mr Pierogi and the Polish Princess, who mingle with the crowds posing for pictures; the Pieroguettes (Miss Mushroom, Miss Plum, Miss Cheese, Miss Potato, Miss Sauerkraut, Miss Chicken, Miss Cabbage, Miss Beef, Miss Apricot, Miss Berry and Miss Chick), who surround Mr Pierogi during the parade; and quite a number of Lil' Dumplings, whose average age is six.

Over in Italy, to reflect the strong links between ingredients, food specialities and the land, innumerable fairs and festivals are organized each year. Traditional foods can be sampled *in loco* while enjoying the local wine, traditional music and dances and the work of contemporary artists. These celebrations of local foods can be a one-day affair, such as Tortellino Day in Bologna, or can last up to a month, like the Festa del Tortello e del Formaggio Artigianale (Tortello and Artisan Cheese Festival) near Florence. However, most fairs last for a weekend or a week, between March and October, and most occur in June, July and August, coinciding with the school holidays and the best weather, allowing all generations to take part in the celebrations well into the night. In Emilia-Romagna one can enjoy the Sagra del Tortellino Tipico at Reno Centese (Ferrara); the Sagra del Tortellino at Castelfranco Emilia (Modena); or the Sagra del Raviolo Dolce at Casalfiumanese (Bologna). The fair in Castelfranco includes the re-enactment of the legend of the tortellino, in medieval costumes, with a local playing the part of the inn-keeper inspired by a beautiful customer to create the stuffed pasta in the shape of her navel. The fair in Casalfiumanese started in 1925 and originally coincided with the much older fair of San Giuseppe, first held in 1738, during which sweet dumplings were given to the children taking part in the celebrations. As a result the tradition has grown up at the Sagra del Raviolo Dolce of throwing dumplings filled with jam and candied fruit to the crowds.

In Veneto the Festa del Nodo d'Amore (Love Knot Fair) takes place at Valeggio sul Mincio (Verona), More than 3,300 people sit at an impressive table over 1 km (½ mile) long to savour tortellini and other local specialities.

In Liguria local women prepare handmade dumplings for the Sagra del Raviolo held at Ceranesi (Genoa). At the Sagra del Raviolo Casalingo at Borgo Fornari (Genoa), only local ingredients from vegetable patches or wild herbs from the

Logo of La Corte dell'Agnolotto Gobbo, an association devoted to the preservation of a traditional recipe from Piedmont, by local artist Antonio Guarene.

countryside are used; while the Sagra del Raviolo di Mare at Marola (La Spezia) celebrates fish and seafood fillings.

Many fairs are also held in Piedmont; they include the Sagra del Raviolo al Plin in Costigliole d'Asti (Asti); the Sagra dell' Agnolotto in Vercelli; the Sagra dell'Agnolotto d'Asino at Calliano (Asti), at which donkey-meat fillings are a speciality; the Sagra dell'Agnolotto Doc at Casale Monferrato (Alessandria); the Sagra dell'Agnolotto e del Canestrello at Polonghera (Cuneo), where filled dumplings are celebrated together with the local chocolate biscuits; the Sagra dell' Agnolotto at Primeglio, Passerano Marmorito (Asti), at Alessandria and also at Pecetto di Valenza (Alessandria); and the Sagra dei Ravioli at Rovereto di Gavi (Alessandria).

In Tuscany it is possible to taste different specialities at the Sagra del Raviolo at Contignano or Radicofani (both in the province of Siena), at Chitignano (Arezzo) or San Vincenzo (Livorno); or at various fairs in or near Florence, where the *tortello*, a rather large type of filled dumpling, is celebrated with *cacciagione* (game) in Borgo San Lorenzo, with *formaggio artigianale* (artisan cheese) in Florence or on its own at Scarperia. Further such festivals take place in many other Italian regions.

Societies and Associations

A typically Italian phenomenon is the presence of a number of associations and societies devoted to the protection and promotion of local ingredients and food specialities, and naturally many are named after specific types of dumpling. Some of the events they organize or participate in have suggestive and entertaining names, including Mani in Pasta (Hands in the Dough) or Festa dell'Affettatrice (Fair of the Meat Slicer).

One such association, the Corte dell'Agnolotto Gobbo (Court of the Hunched Dumpling), was founded in 2006 by a small group of friends. Its purpose is to record and preserve the traditional Piedmont recipes for *agnolotto gobbo*, which originated in the region around Asti, and to differentiate it from the *agnolotto al plin*, also rigorously made by hand but slightly different and increasing in popularity across the region. The original recipe for *agnolotto gobbo* was registered at the Council of Asti and granted a Denominazione Comunale (denomination of council origin; De.Co.) as a result of the Court's activities.

The Ordine Obertengo dei Cavalieri del Raviolo e del Gavi (Order of the Ravioli Knights), meanwhile, inspired by

Giant monument to the dumpling in the village of Glendon, Alberta, Canada.

medieval ceremonies, has been operating in Gavi since 1973, and organizes events, activities and themed dinners to promote the original handmade ravioli from Gavi.

Monuments

One of the ways in which dumplings are celebrated elsewhere in the world is with unusual monuments. In Glendon, Alberta, Canada, there is a giant monument to the Ukrainian dumpling held by an equally giant fork, while in Poltava, Ukraine, there is a large sculpture of the local bran dumplings with a giant bowl and ladle. A similar monument in Cherkasy, Ukraine, shows Cossack Mamay, a Ukrainian folklore character well-known for his fondness for *varenyky*, eating from an earthenware pot while comfortably sitting on a giant crescent-shaped dumpling.

6

How to Make Dumplings

Preparing most types of dumpling requires only a work surface and rolling pin. However, there are some utensils that can make the task of preparing the wrappers for certain types of filled dumpling either easier or quicker, or both: among them a pasta machine, a ravioli cutting tray, a ravioli cutter and a zigzag cutter wheel. A colander or coarse grater can be useful for preparing German *Spätzle* or Hungarian *nokedli*.

Despite the fact that most pasta is bought dry or in vacuum packs, many Italian households still own a pasta machine. The sheets of dough produced using this method are smoother, more even and often thinner than if hand-rolled, and make ideal wrappers for homemade ravioli.

A ravioli cutting tray is a rectangular metal or plastic tray that usually has twelve or 24 indentations which are deep enough to hold small balls of filling and separated by zigzag edges. A sheet of pasta is placed on the tray and the filling spooned into each hollow. A second sheet of pasta is then laid on top of the first before pressure is exerted using a rolling pin to seal and cut the edges simultaneously. Cutting trays can be rather awkward to use, as the pasta can easily stick to the tray if the filling is even just slightly moister than it should be.

Common utensils for making dumplings include a rolling pin, a pasta machine, a ravioli cutting tray and a zigzag cutter wheel.

Filled dumplings can be made in different shapes: squares, circles and hearts are all common. While simple cookie cutters can be used, special ravioli cutters are available that differ by having a handle and, usually, a zigzag edge.

A zigzag cutter wheel is probably the simplest and easiest option for cutting dumplings, after a sharp knife. It is smaller than the cutting wheel used to cut pizza into slices, and has a zigzag blade that gives ravioli its typical toothed edge.

As boiled dumplings can easily fall apart, they must be handled with care. Skimmers or slotted spoons are helpful for draining them, especially the most delicate ones, so they do not break.

For steaming dumplings one can use Western or Asian steamer baskets made of metal or bamboo. Plastic steamers are also available for use in microwave ovens.

Wonton preparation with ready-made wrappers and bean paste filling.

Shaping, Filling and Folding Techniques

The shape and size of dumplings vary depending on whether they have a filling or not, and also according to the region, the cooking method and the skill of the cook. The illustration on p. 13 shows some traditional and common shapes.

Unfilled dumplings are usually quick and easy to shape, but the filling and folding of filled dumplings require a certain level of skill and a fair amount of practice. The following explanations and diagrams provide an overview of some of the techniques used in different parts of the world to obtain different types of dumpling.

The typical shape of many unfilled dumplings, including British floating dumplings and *canederli* from northern Italy, is a simple ball. To make a dumpling like this, fill your cupped palm with the dumpling mixture and with the help of the other hand roll it into a regularly shaped ball.

Tips for First-timers

Regardless of the type of filled dumpling, there are
a few tips that will most certainly come in useful.

The filling should be firm. Runny, wet fillings
will cause trouble by:
– running from the centre to the edges of the wrapper,
preventing them from sticking together;
– wetting the dough through and making it stick to
the work surface and tray.

The dough should be worked long enough for it to become
elastic.

The dough should be rolled into sheets as thin as required
by the recipe or the wrapping will be too prominent and
hard, even when thoroughly cooked through, and will
detract from the flavour of the filling.

Just before folding the dough around the filling and
pressing or pinching the edges together, it is useful to
dip a finger in cold water and run it along the edges
of the wrapper; this will prevent the filling from
escaping during cooking.

Dumplings grow when boiled or steamed, so sufficient
space should be allowed in the pan or steamer.

The Italian potato gnocchi and the smaller wheat-based
pisarei are in the shape of a little lump, hollowed out with the
help of a fork to make it lighter and more suited to scooping
up the accompanying sauce. To make a dumpling in this shape,
roll the mixture into a sausage and cut into equal pieces. One by

one, gently push each piece against the concave face of a fork, creating a small indentation with your thumb at the same time.

Italian ravioli and German *Maultaschen* are among the filled dumplings with regular square or rectangular shapes. Place small balls of filling, the size of a hazelnut, on a sheet of thinly rolled dough, in horizontal rows a couple of fingers apart. Place a second sheet of pasta on top and press with your fingers around each ball of filling until the pasta layers are in contact. With a sharp knife or zigzag cutter wheel, cut decisively through the dough following the invisible grid to separate the dumplings. Finally, check the dumplings one by one to make sure the filling is completely sealed within the pasta.

Eastern European filled dumplings, including Russian *pelmeni* and Polish *pierogi*, often have a chunky half-moon or crested oval shape. Cut circles out of a thin sheet of dough using a glass or a large cookie cutter, and place a small ball of filling in the middle of each circle. For a chunky half-moon shape, fold the circle in two and pinch the edges together, creating an attractive pattern with your fingers. To make a crested oval shape, hold the half-moon dumpling by its ridge, roll it over by 90 degrees and gently push down until the dumpling sits on top of its own filling.

The typical shape of Italian tortellini, Chinese *chāoshŏu* (literally 'crossed hands') and some Ukranian *varenyky* is a ring, reminding one of a navel. Cut squares out of a thin sheet of dough using a sharp knife or cutting wheel. Place a small ball of filling in the middle of each square, then fold the square in two and press the edges together to seal the filling inside. Hold the dumpling in your left hand with your thumb lightly touching the top of the dumpling. With your right hand fold two corners together, then slide your left thumb out from underneath the dough.

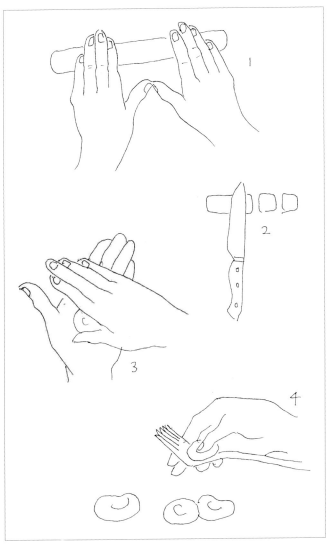

Method of making gnocchi.

Turkish *manti* and some types of Chinese wonton come in the shape of satchels or drawstring bags. Cut squares out of a thin sheet of dough using a sharp knife or cutting wheel. Place a small ball of filling in the middle of each square. Bring the four corners together and press the inner edges of the square firmly together to obtain dumplings in the shape of a parcel. For the look of a drawstring bag, slightly twist the top of the dumpling.

The typical shape of the Mongolian *buuz* is that of a dome with elaborate pleats at the top, around a steaming hole. The size, shape and number of folds largely depend on the skill and patience of the cook. Roll small pieces of dough into circles, and, holding each one in the palm of one hand, place a teaspoon of filling in the centre. Fold the edges at one end and press them together between your index finger and thumb. Make another fold next to the previous one and press the edges together. Continue along the dumpling, rotating it as you go. When the last fold is complete you should be left with a hole at the top, through which the steam can escape.

Broths, Sauces and Condiments

Unfilled dumplings are served in broth, in a stew or accompanied by gravy or a rich sauce. Stuffed dumplings, on the other hand, tend to be served with the simplest of sauces or dipping condiments. Chicken broth is a very popular choice of liquid in which to serve dumplings, but as a general rule the broth matches the filling, with seafood dumplings cooked and served in a fish or seaweed broth, and vegetable dumplings usually served in a vegetable broth. Accompanying sauces vary according to the type of dumpling and its size, shape and provenance. Italian vegetable dumplings are often served with sage and

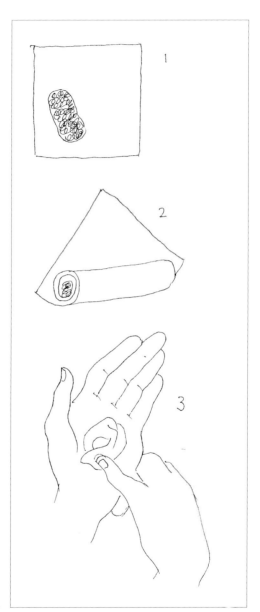

Method of
making tortellini.

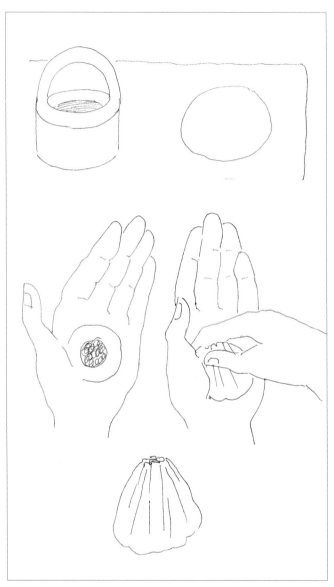

Method of making *buuz*.

Making Mongolian *buuz*: cutting the dough into even pieces; filling the dough; wrapping the filling; dumplings ready for steaming.

melted butter, while meaty ones can be accompanied by thick tomato sauces or meat and tomato ragú. In Central Asia dumplings are often covered in warm yoghurt flavoured with garlic and herbs, while in Central and Eastern Europe they tend to be served with a dollop of sour cream and sprinkled with fried onions. Asian dumplings, whether boiled or steamed, are often served with dipping sauces and condiments based on soy sauce or chilli oil.

Colourful Wrappers

In many cuisines, colouring ingredients are added to the dough to give some colour to the wrappers. For example, colourful dumplings are served as part of lavish Chinese dim sum, and in Italy, around carnival time (just before the beginning of Lent), it is possible to find multicoloured harlequin dumplings made by sealing meat-based fillings between two layers of dough of different colours. The quantity of colouring ingredients varies according to the type and quality of the flour. If the colouring ingredient contains a certain amount of water, for example puréed spinach, carrot, beetroot or squid ink, more flour is needed than indicated in the usual recipe. Here are some ways to obtain colourful egg- and flour-based wrappers, based on a recipe that uses 200 g flour.

Green: 1 egg and 100 g fresh spinach, boiled, drained, squeezed and puréed or very finely chopped

Orange: 1 egg and 100 g carrots, boiled and puréed

Purple: 1 egg and 100 g beetroot or red cabbage, boiled and puréed

Pink: small eggs and a tablespoonful of tomato purée (paste)

Black: 2 small eggs and a sachet of squid ink

Yellow: 1–2 g saffron flowers or 1 tsp curry powder or turmeric, to be mixed with the flour before adding 2 medium eggs

Brown: a tablespoonful of dark (unsweetened) cocoa powder, to be mixed with the flour before adding 2 medium eggs

Green, red or black speckles: add to the dough a couple of tablespoonfuls of finely chopped herbs, such as rosemary, sage, coriander (cilantro) or parsley; some mild, deseeded chilli, finely chopped; or coarsely ground black pepper

Recipes

Savoury Dumplings

Tortellini in Brodo (Italian Dumplings in Broth)

For the dough
600 g plain (all-purpose) flour
6 eggs

For the filling
150 g pork meat, shallow-fried in butter
150 g Parma ham
150 g mortadella
150 g Parmesan cheese, grated
1 egg
grated nutmeg
2 litres stock

Mix the flour and eggs in a large bowl and knead until the dough is elastic in texture. Leave to rest, covered with a tea towel, while you prepare the filling. Place all the ingredients for the filling in a food processor and blend to obtain a homogeneous and firm mixture. Follow the method on page 101 to make about 120 ring-shaped dumplings. Boil in the stock for 5–7 minutes and serve in the cooking liquid.

Serves 12

Ravioli di Magro
(Italian Dumplings with Spinach and Ricotta Cheese)

For the dough
400 g plain (all-purpose) flour
4 eggs

For the filling
400 g spinach
1 egg yolk
250 g ricotta cheese
4 tbsp grated Parmesan cheese, plus extra to serve (optional)
olive oil, to serve (optional)
melted butter and sage, to serve (optional)

Mix the flour and eggs in a large bowl and knead until the dough is elastic in texture. Leave to rest, covered with a tea towel, while you prepare the filling. To make the filling, boil the spinach in water for a few minutes and squeeze dry. Add the egg yolk and the cheeses and mix thoroughly. Follow the method on page 98 to make about 60 square dumplings. Drop the dumplings into boiling water, cook for a few minutes, drain and serve with a drizzle of olive oil and extra Parmesan cheese, or with melted butter and sage.
Serves 6

Tortelli di Zucca (Italian Dumplings with Pumpkin)

For the dough
400 g plain (all-purpose) flour
4 eggs

For the filling
400 g peeled and diced pumpkin
75 g amaretto biscuits, crushed
breadcrumbs, if required
olive oil and grated Parmesan cheese, to serve

Mix the flour and eggs in a large bowl and knead until the dough is elastic in texture. Leave to rest, covered with a tea towel, while you prepare the filling. For the filling, boil the pumpkin in about 100 ml of water for 15–20 minutes, until very soft. Drain and mash with a fork or potato masher, or in a food processor. Add the amaretto biscuits and, if the mixture is too wet, a couple of teaspoons of breadcrumbs to absorb the excess liquid, and season. Follow the method on page 99 to make about 40 large square dumplings. Drop the dumplings into boiling water, cook for a few minutes, drain and serve with a drizzle of olive oil and Parmesan cheese.

Serves 6

Canederli allo Speck
(Round Dumplings with Smoked Bacon)

2 eggs
500 ml milk
600 g stale bread, cut into cubes
1 small onion, chopped
3 tbsp olive oil
200 g speck, cut into small cubes
4 tbsp parsley, chopped
80 g plain (all-purpose) flour
grated nutmeg
1½ litres stock
salt and freshly ground black pepper

Mix the eggs and milk in a large bowl, add the bread, season and leave to rest for about an hour. Meanwhile, fry the onion in a pan with the olive oil, add the speck and cook for about 5 minutes. Allow to cool before adding to the bread mixture together with the parsley, flour and nutmeg. Mix well, then shape into balls the size of an egg. Bring the broth to the boil and add the dumplings one by one. Cook for about 15 minutes. Serve three or four *canederli* per person, in the broth.

Serves 8

Gnocchi al Gorgonzola
(Potato Dumplings with Cheese Sauce)

For the gnocchi
1½ kg potatoes
1 egg
280 g plain (all-purpose) flour, plus extra if required

For the sauce
200 g gorgonzola or blue cheese
200 ml milk
2 tbsp plain (all-purpose) flour

Cook the potatoes in boiling water for about 40 minutes, until soft, then peel, mash and leave to cool. Add the egg and flour to the potatoes and knead the mixture, adding a little more flour if the dough is too sticky. Follow the method on page 98 to make small hollow dumplings. For the sauce, heat the cheese and milk in a pan over very low heat until the cheese is melted. Add the flour and stir well until thickened. Drop the dumplings into boiling water and cook for a few minutes, until they float to the surface. Drain and serve hot with the cheese sauce.
Serves 6

Chinese Wontons with Pork and Shrimp

200 g lean pork
200 g shelled prawns (shrimp)
about 3 cm piece fresh ginger
1 tbsp oyster sauce
2 tsp soy sauce
1 tbsp rice vinegar
1 tsp sugar
1 tsp sesame oil
1½ litres clear stock
30 ready-made wonton wrappers

Finely chop the pork and prawns (shrimp). Peel and chop the ginger. Mix the pork and prawns with the ginger, oyster sauce, soy sauce, rice vinegar, sugar and sesame oil. Follow the method on page 100 to make dumplings in the shape of satchels. Boil the dumplings in the broth for about 5–8 minutes, until they rise to the top and the filling is cooked through. Remove from the pan with a slotted spoon and serve in the broth.

Serves 6

Chinese *Baozi* with Cabbage, Beetroot and Ginger

For the dough
2 sachets (6 g each) active dry yeast
up to 500 ml warm water
400 g plain (all-purpose) flour
50 g sugar
1 tbsp cooking oil
1 ½ tsp baking powder

For the filling
300 g cabbage, finely chopped
300 g beetroot, finely diced
1 large ginger root, peeled and finely chopped
1 tbsp sesame oil
2 tbsp soy sauce
1 tsp sugar
1 tsp rice wine

Dissolve the yeast in the water and add flour, sugar and oil. Knead until smooth and leave the dough to rest for about 45 minutes, until it has doubled in size. Flatten the dough with a rolling pin, sprinkle the baking powder on top, fold in two and knead again. Divide into 18 equal-sized balls and leave to rest for about 30 minutes more, until it has again grown in size. Meanwhile, blanch the cabbage in boiling water, drain and mix with the other filling ingredients. Follow the method on page 102 to make dumplings in the shape of small buns. Leave the filled dumplings to rest and rise for about 30 minutes. Bring water to the boil in a steamer and arrange the dumplings on baking paper or cabbage leaves to prevent them from sticking to the basket. Steam for about 10 minutes over a high heat, and serve hot.

Serves 6

Russian *Pelmeni* with Beef and Pork

For the filling
250 g minced (ground) beef
250 g minced (ground) pork
1 onion, finely chopped
salt and freshly ground black pepper

For the dough
280 g plain (all-purpose) flour
3 eggs
110 ml milk or water
a little vegetable oil

melted butter or sour cream, to serve

Prepare the filling by mixing the beef and pork with the onion and salt and pepper. Set aside. For the dough, mix the flour, eggs and milk or water, add a pinch of salt and a drop of oil and knead on a floured surface until elastic. Follow the method on page 98 to make about 24 dumplings in the shape of chunky half-moons. Cook the dumplings in boiling water for 10–15 minutes, until the dough is soft. Drain and serve with melted butter or a generous dollop of sour cream.

Serves 4

Polish *Pierogi* with Sauerkraut and Mushrooms

For the filling
200 g fresh mushrooms (or 40 g dried)
1 onion
a knob (pat) of butter
400 g sauerkraut, rinsed and drained
50 g plain (all-purpose) flour
salt and freshly ground black pepper

For the dough
280 g plain (all-purpose) flour
2 eggs
110 ml water

melted butter and fried onions, to serve

If using dried mushrooms, soak them in warm water for about an hour before starting. For the filling, fry the mushrooms and onion in the butter for a few minutes, add the sauerkraut and cook for 10 minutes. Mix the flour with a little water, add to the other ingredients and simmer for 15 minutes. Season with salt and pepper to taste, and set aside. Place the flour for the dough in a heap on a work surface and make a well in the centre. Break the eggs into the well and mix with the flour. Add the water and a pinch of salt and knead until firm and elastic. Leave the dough to rest for 15 minutes, covered with a cloth. Follow the method on page 98 to make about 24 dumplings in the shape of chunky half-moons. Cook the dumplings in salted boiling water for 5–10 minutes. Drain and serve with melted butter and fried onions.
Serves 4

Turkish *Manti* with Yoghurt and Garlic Sauce

For the dough
280 g plain (all-purpose) flour
1 egg, lightly beaten
60 ml water
salt

For the filling
500 g minced (ground) beef
1 onion, finely chopped
parsley

For the yoghurt and garlic sauce
450 ml yoghurt
3 tsp finely chopped garlic

Prepare the dough by putting the flour in a mixing bowl, making a well in the centre and adding the egg and water and a pinch of salt. Work the ingredients together until they form a dough, and knead until smooth and elastic. Cover and leave to rest for an hour. Prepare the filling by mixing the beef, onion and parsley and a pinch of salt in a bowl. For the sauce, combine the yoghurt and garlic in a small bowl and leave at room temperature until ready to serve. Follow the method on page 100 to make dumplings in the shape of rings or drawstring bags. Bring a large pan of water to the boil and drop in the dumplings. They will rise to the surface as soon as they are cooked. Drain and place in a serving dish. Cover with the yoghurt sauce and sprinkle with red pepper powder.
Serves 4

Chicken 'n' Dumplings

4 chicken breasts, diced
3 tbsp plain (all-purpose) flour
2 tbsp vegetable oil
2 carrots, sliced
2 sticks of celery, sliced
2 potatoes, diced
1 onion, chopped
1 litre chicken stock
225 ml milk
1 tsp rosemary
1 tsp sage
150 g self-raising flour
50 g shredded suet
salt and freshly ground black pepper

Coat the chicken in the plain flour and season with salt and pepper. Heat the oil in a large casserole dish and fry the chicken for a few minutes, then add the vegetables. Pour in the chicken stock and milk and add half the herbs. Bring to the boil, cover and simmer for 10 minutes. In a bowl, mix the self-raising flour, suet and the remaining herbs. Season and add 6 tbsp water to form a soft dough. Divide the dough into 6 balls and place on top of the mixture in the casserole dish. Cover and cook for 25 minutes, until the dumplings are firm.
Serves 6

Norfolk Dumplings

2 tsp fresh yeast
1 tsp caster (superfine) sugar
¼ pint warm water
560 g plain (all-purpose) flour
150 ml milk

melted butter, meat stew and gravy, to serve

Mix the yeast, sugar and water and leave to stand for 10 minutes, until frothy. Place the flour in a bowl and add the milk and the yeast mixture. Mix and leave for about 1½ hours to rise. Knead the dough well, form into round dumplings and leave to stand for about 10 minutes. Drop the dumplings into a pan of boiling water and cook for about 20 minutes. Serve hot, with melted butter, meat stew and gravy.

Serves 6

Fufu and *Maafe*
(African Dumplings with Peanut Soup)

For the dumplings
1 yam
1 plantain

For the peanut soup
2 chicken breasts, diced
1 tomato, chopped
1 small onion, finely chopped
2 garlic cloves, finely chopped
1 stock (bouillon) cube
150 g peanut butter
2 tbsp tomato purée (paste)
2 tsp vegetable oil
salt and freshly ground black pepper

Boil the yam and plantain in water for about 30 minutes, until soft. Peel and mash until very smooth. Shape into balls roughly the size of tennis balls. Put the chicken, tomato, onion and garlic into a casserole dish. Add the stock (bouillon) cube and 225 ml water and season. Cover and boil for about 15 minutes on a medium heat. Add the peanut butter and a further 450 ml water. Stir, cover and cook for about 10 minutes. Add the tomato purée (paste) and oil and serve hot accompanied by the *fufu* dumplings.

Serves 4

Dessert Dumplings

Turogomboc
(Hungarian Cheese Dumplings with Jam)

400 g cottage cheese
3 eggs, lightly beaten
135 g semolina
1 tbsp butter
50 g breadcrumbs
1 tbsp caster (superfine) sugar
110 ml sour cream, 90 g jam and icing (confectioners')
sugar, to serve

Mix the cheese with the eggs and add the semolina. Cover and refrigerate for at least an hour. Bring a pot of salted water to the boil. Wet your hands and shape the cheese mixture into balls, using about 2 tbsp mixture per dumpling. Drop the dumplings into boiling water, cook for 5–10 minutes and lift out with a slotted spoon. Melt the butter in a frying pan, add the breadcrumbs and caster sugar, stir gently until lightly browned and remove from the heat. Roll the dumplings in the breadcrumb mixture until fully coated. Serve with a spoonful of sour cream and half a spoonful of jam, and sprinkled with icing (confectioner's) sugar.
Serves 4

Ravioli with Chocolate filling and Orange Sauce

For the dough
200 g plain (all-purpose) flour
3 egg yolks
40 ml cold water

For the filling
half a square of dark or milk chocolate for each dumpling

For the orange sauce
2 large oranges
50 g sugar

Mix the flour, egg yolks and water in a large bowl and knead until
the dough is elastic in texture. Leave to rest, covered with a tea
towel, for about 30 minutes. Follow the method on page 98 to
make 20 square dumplings filled with the chocolate, and store in
the refrigerator. Prepare the orange sauce by placing the grated peel
and juice of the oranges in a pan with the sugar. Boil until thick
and partially caramelized. To serve, drop the dumplings, straight
from the fridge, into boiling water. Cook for a few minutes, drain
and serve hot with a drizzle of orange sauce.
Serves 4

Hanami Dango
(Japanese Sweet Rice-flour Dumplings)

140 g mochiko rice flour
75 ml boiling water
3 tbsp strawberry pureé (pink)
1 tbsp matcha powder (green)

Mix the rice flour and water to obtain a firm but slightly crumbly
dough. Divide equally between three small bowls. In the first
bowl, mix the dough with the strawberry pureé; in the second
bowl, mix the dough with the matcha powder; and leave the third
part of the dough uncoloured. Roll into balls about 3 cm in diam-
eter. Cook the dumplings in boiling water until they rise to the
surface. Drain, and drop into iced water to cool. Place one
dumpling of each colour on a skewer, and serve immediately.
Serves 5

Glossary

Agnoli: Italian filled dumplings from the Lombardy region

Agnolotti: Italian filled dumplings from the Piedmont region; can be *gobbi* (hunchback) or *al plin* (pinched), depending on the folding method

Anolini: Italian filled dumplings from the town of Parma

Bánh bao: Vietnamese filled steamed bun, similar to Chinese *baozi*

Banku: West African steamed dumpling

Bansh: Boiled Mongolian dumpling filled with meat and shaped as a half-moon

Baozi: Chinese filled steamed bun made from a fluffy, bread-like dough

Boller: Small Danish flour dumpling served in broth or thick soup

Bramborové knedlíky: Czech potato dumpling

Bryndzové pirohy: Slovak dumpling filled with salty cheese

Buuz: Steamed Mongolian dumpling filled with meat and shaped into a dome with a hole at the top

Calzoncelli: Italian filled dumplings from the region of Puglia

Canederli: Large boiled ball-shaped dumplings from northern Italy

Cappellacci: Italian filled dumplings from the town of Ferrara

Cappelletti: Italian filled dumplings from the town of Modena

Caramelle: Italian filled dumplings from the town of Piacenza, shaped as wrapped boiled sweets

Casoncelli: Italian filled dumplings from the town of Brescia

Cepelinai: Lithuanian large oblong potato dumpling

Cha siu baau: Chinese steamed dumpling filled with barbeque-flavoured pork

Chāoshǒu: Chinese steamed dumpling shaped as 'crossed hands' or tortellini

Chuchvara: Small dumpling from Uzbekistan, filled with minced meat and shaped like Italian tortellini

Cialzons: Italian filled dumplings from the Carnia region

Csipetke: Hungarian flour dumpling served in broth or thick soup

Culingiones or **Cullurzones:** Italian filled dumplings from Sardinia

Derelye: Hungarian dumpling filled with meat or jam

Doushabao: Chinese dumpling filled with sweet bean paste

Dushbara: Boiled dumpling from Azerbaijan, filled with lamb and shaped like Italian tortellini

Fagotti: Italian filled dumplings

Fagottini: Small Italian filled dumplings

Fazzoletti: Large Italian filled dumplings

Fufu: African steamed dumpling made from yam or cassava and served with soup or stew

Fun guo: Chinese filled steamed dumpling made of a thick wrapper and filled with minced pork, dried shrimp and peanuts

Germknödel: German sweet steamed dumpling filled with jam or fruit compote

Gnocchi: Small, firm Italian potato dumpling

Gnocchi alla Romana: Soft Italian semolina dumpling cooked with cheese and butter

Gomboc: Hungarian large boiled dumpling

Guanimes rellenos: large dumplings made from maize flour and filled with meat, popular in Puerto Rico

Guotie (pot-sticker)**:** Chinese filled dumpling made of a thick dough, shaped like a crescent moon and cooked in a pan

Gundi: Small Jewish dumpling made from egg and flour and added to chicken soup in the Ashkenazi tradition

Gunmandu: Korean filled dumpling, similar to Chinese *guotie*

Gyoza: Japanese filled dumpling very similar to Chinese *jiaozi*

Hayacas: Large dumplings made of maize flour and filled with meat or cheese, popular in Colombia, Venezuela and Equador

Har gow: Chinese filled steamed dumpling made with very thin wrappers and served as dim sum

Humitas: Peruvian large dumplings made of maize flour and filled with meat or cheese

Jiaozi: Chinese filled dumpling made of a thick and chewy dough, and shaped like a fat crescent moon

Kalduny: Belarusian boiled dumpling filled with meat, mushrooms or cheese

Kams: Norwegian potato dumpling

Kartoffelknödel: German potato dumpling with egg and bacon, served with meats

Kenkey: West African steamed dumpling made of fermented maize

Khinkali: Georgian and Azerbaijani dumpling filled with spiced meat

Khuushuur: Pan-fried Mongolian dumpling filled with meat and shaped as a half-moon

Klim: Small Swedish flour dumpling served in broth or thick soup

Kløbb: Norwegian potato dumpling

Klot: Norwegian potato dumpling

Klösse: Large dumpling, popular in Germany, Austria and Switzerland, boiled in water or broth

Kluski: Polish large cheese dumpling

Knaidl: Jewish dumpling made of matza meal and shaped into a large ball

Knedle od sljiva: Croatian potato dumpling with plum filling

Knedliki: Czech large boiled dumpling

Knödel: Large dumpling, popular in Germany, Austria and Switzerland, boiled in water or broth

Knodli: Hungarian small dumpling made of flour, egg and water, served as a side dish

Komle: Norwegian potato dumpling

Kompe: Norwegian potato dumpling

Komperdøse: Norwegian potato dumpling

Kopytka: Polish potato dumpling

Kreplach: Jewish dumpling filled with ground meat or mashed potatoes and served in a broth

Kromme: Norwegian potato dumpling

Kroppkakor: Swedish potato dumpling

Kudle: Norwegian potato dumpling

Lazy varenyky: Russian and Ukrainian small boiled dumpling made with fresh cheese, egg and flour

Malfatti: Small Italian boiled dumpling made with flour, egg and cheese and also known as 'naked ravioli'

Manapua: Hawaiian filled steamed bun, similar to Chinese *baozi*

Mandu: Korean filled dumpling similar to Chinese *jiaozi*

Mangu: Steamed plantain dumpling from the Dominican Republic

Manti: boiled dumpling from Turkey, Central Asia and parts of the Middle East, filled with lamb or chicken and topped with yoghurt and garlic, also known as *Tatar böregi* (Tartar pasties)

Mantou: Chinese steamed bun made from a fluffy, bread-like dough

Mantu: Dumpling from Afghanistan filled with ground lamb and served with yoghurt

Marillenknödel: Large round potato dumpling with fruit filling, popular in Germany, Austria and Switzerland

Marubini: Italian filled dumpling from the town of Cremona

Maultaschen: Large filled dumpling from southwest Germany, made of a wheat-dough wrapper filled with meat or vegetables

Mofongo: Steamed plantain dumpling from Cuba and Puerto Rico

Momo: Steamed or boiled dumpling popular in Tibet and Nepal

Nikuman: Japanese filled steamed bun, very similar to Chinese *baozi*

Nsima: Steamed dumpling popular in Malawi

Nzema or **Nshima:** Zambian steamed dumpling

Pansotti: Italian filled dumplings from the Liguria region

Panzerotti: Italian filled dumplings from the town of Naples

Pap: South African steamed dumpling

Pastelle: Large meat-filled dumplings made from maize flour, popular in Trinidad and Tobago

Pastillitos: Large meat-filled dumplings made from maize flour, popular in the Dominican Republic

Pegai: Italian filled dumplings from the town of Parma

Pelmeni: Russian filled boiled dumpling made from flour dough and meat or vegetable filling

Pierogi: Polish filled boiled dumpling made from a flour wrapper and meat, cheese, potato or sweet filling

Posho: Ugandan steamed dumpling

Potetball: Norwegian potato dumpling

Raskekako: Norwegian potato dumpling

Raspeball: Norwegian potato dumpling

Ravaiuoli: Italian filled dumplings from the Irpinia region

Ravioli: Italian dumpling made of a filling wrapped in pasta dough

Ravjul: Maltese dumpling similar to ravioli, filled with cheese

Ruta: Norwegian potato dumpling

Sadza: Steamed dumpling very popular in Zimbabwe

Salapao: Thai filled steamed bun, similar to Chinese *baozi*

Semmel Knödel: German dumpling made of stale bread flavoured with cheese or mushrooms

Shish barak: Lebanese boiled dumpling filled with minced meat and served in a yoghurt sauce

Siopao: filipino steamed filled bun, similar to Chinese *baozi*

Souskluitjies: South African sweet boiled dumpling served with syrup

Spätzle: Small dumpling made of flour, egg and water, served with meat and stews and popular in Germany, Switzerland and Austria

Strozzapreti: Small Italian dumplings made from flour, egg and water, served with a thick tomato sauce

Szilvas gomboc: Hungarian potato dumpling with plum filling

Tamales: Latin American large dumplings made from maize flour and filled with meat or cheese

Tordelli: Italian filled dumplings from the town of Lucca

Tortelli: Italian filled dumplings

Tortellini: Ring-shaped Italian filled dumplings

Tortelloni: Large Italian filled dumplings

Turogomboc: Hungarian large round dumpling with cheese

Ugali: South and east African steamed dumpling made with maize flour

Uszka: small Polish dumpling filled with mushrooms and served in broth

Varenyky: Ukrainian filled boiled dumpling made of wheat dough with a meat, vegetable or sweet filling

Wonton: Chinese filled dumpling made from a thin dough wrapper and usually steamed or served in broth

Xiaolongbao: Chinese small, meat-filled steamed bun containing a juicy broth

Yaki-gyoza: Japanese filled dumpling, very similar to similar to Chinese *guotie*

Zwetschgenknödel: Large round potato dumpling with plum filling, popular in Germany, Austria, Switzerland, Poland and Romania

Select Bibliography

Anon., *La Cuciniera Piemontese* (Vercelli, Italy, 1771)

Artusi, Pellegrino, *La Scienza in cucina e l'arte di mangier bene* (Florence, 2003), in English as *Science in the Kitchen and the Art of Eating Well*, trans. Murtha Baca and Stephen Sartarelli (Toronto, ON, 2003)

Beeton, Isabella, *The Book of Household Management* (London, 1861)

Blot, Pierre, *Hand-book of Practical Cookery, for Ladies and the Professional Cooks: Containing the Whole Science and Art of Preparing Human Food* (New York, 1884)

Botti, Ferruccio, *Gastronomia Parmense* (Parma, Italy, 1952)

Consiglio, Alberto, *La Storia dei maccheroni* (Rome, 1948)

Davidson, Alan, *The Oxford Companion to Food* (Oxford, 1999; 2nd edn 2006)

Fra Salimbene de Adam, *Cronica* [*c.* 1282–7] (Hanover, 1905)

Francatelli, Charles Elmé, *A Plain Cookery Book for the Working Classes* (London, 1852)

Gillette, F. L., and Hugo Ziemann, *The White House Cook Book* (New York, 1887)

Goudiss, C. Houston, and Alberta M. Goudiss, *Foods that Will Win the War and How to Cook Them* (New York, 1918)

Guaiti, Daniela, *La Grande Cucina regionale italiana: Emilia Romagna* (Milan, 2010)

Gundel, Károly, *Gundel's Hungarian Cookbook* (Budapest, 1956; 31st edn 2008)

Hardy, Sheila, *Arsenic in the Dumplings: A Casebook of Historic Poisonings in Suffolk* (Stroud, Gloucestershire, 2010)

Hom, Ken, *Chinese Cookery*, new edn (London, 2009)

Kenedy, Jacob, and Caz Hildebrand, *The Geometry of Pasta* (London, 2010)

Polushkin, Maria, *The Dumpling Cookbook* (New York, 1977)

Quaini, Massimo, *Per la Storia del paesaggio agrario in Liguria* (Genoa, Italy, 1972)

Roden, Claudia, *The Book of Jewish Food: An Odyssey from Samarkand and Vilna to the Present Day* (London, 1997)

——, *A New Book of Middle Eastern Food* (Harmondsworth, 1986)

Whorton, James C., *The Arsenic Century: How Victorian Britain was Poisoned at Home, Work and Play* (Oxford, 2010)

Yarvin, Brian, *A World of Dumplings: Filled Dumplings, Pockets, and Little Pies from Around the Globe* (Woodstock, VT, 2007)

Websites and Associations

European culinary and dietetic texts
from the Middle Ages to 1800
www.uni-giessen.de/gloning/kobu.htm

Children's films on African food
www.our-africa.org/foods

Life and recipes of Pellegrino Artusi
www.pellegrinoartusi.it

Corte dell'Agnolotto Gobbo
Association established to preserve the
traditional recipe for this dumpling
www.agnolottogobbo.it

Official site of the Whiting Pierogi Fest
www.pierogifest.net

Official site of the Pittsburgh Pirates and Pierogi Race
http://pittsburgh.pirates.mlb.com

Story of the Italian ravioli manufacturer Giovanni Rana
www.giovannirana.com/story

My Favourite Blogs

Little Italy and a Bit More
Lovely recipes for *tortelli*, gnocchi, *Spätzle* and *canederli*
www.littleitalyandabitmore.blogspot.co.uk

Tiny Urban Kitchen
Asian recipes
www.tinyurbankitchen.com

My Kitchen Table
Includes a video of making ravioli
www.mykitchentable.co.uk

Pierogi Fest
Programme and pictures
www.pierogifest.net

Acknowledgements

I love food, and writing this book was a real pleasure, although it meant many nights and long solitary weekends researching the subject in libraries and bookshops, trying out recipes in the kitchen and typing away on my laptop. I could not have done it without the encouragement and support of Chris, my husband, who found the time in between tennis, judo and songwriting to photograph dumplings and proofread my manuscript. Alison Booth, travel writer and zumba enthusiast, gave me the last push over the finishing line, and I am very grateful for her patience and thoughtful advice. The beautiful drawings were executed by my close friend Emma Harris and by artist Lucy Rickards. My sister Silvia and my parents also contributed photographs, tales and recipes to this project.

I then want to thank literary agent Brie Burkeman, who introduced me to many relevant books by cookery experts, and Lulu Grimes, food director of *Olive* and *BBC Good Food* magazines, who was my teacher at Leiths School of Food and Wine in London and gave me an invaluable introduction to the world of publishing.

I also thank my friends Hanne, Manola, Jess, Kate, Michelle, Sandra, Maureen and all the dinner guests who tested many of my trial recipes for dumplings and sauces.

Photo Acknowledgements

The author and the publishers wish to express their thanks to the below sources of illustrative material and/or permission to reproduce it.

© The Trustees of the British Museum: pp. 38, 40, 41, 42; Photo-China Daily: p. 85; Chris Dixon: pp. 9, 19, 24, 26, 28, 50, 54–5, 62, 65, 66, 68, 76; Chris Dixon (photography)/Barbara Gallani (food preparation and food styling): pp. 18, 20, 23, 30, 33, 45, 57, 59, 60, 95, 96; courtesy of Count Enzenberg, copyright Gregor Khuen Belasi: p. 35; Barbara Gallani: pp. 8, 72; Silvia Gallani: p. 48; courtesy of Antonio Guarene: p. 90; Emma Harris: pp. 16–17, 73; courtesy of ITALGI s.r.l: p. 11; Michael Leaman: p. 103; Malo: p. 86; copyright Pierogi Fest, Whiting, In.: p. 87; Rex Features: p. 82 (Snap Stills); Lucy Rickards: pp. 13, 99, 101, 102; Shutterstock: p. 6 (Gianluca Foto); Victoria & Albert Museum, London: p. 25; courtesy of Village of Glendon, Alberta, Canada: p. 92.

Index

italic numbers refer to illustrations; **bold** to recipes